Facilitating Collective Intelligence

Chantal Nève-Hanquet and Agathe Crespel provide an accessible and ground-breaking guide to genuinely effective group work, sharing excellent hands-on assistance for coaches and facilitators. Offering a unique selection of guidelines and illustrations for group work, the authors demonstrate the benefits of using creative action methods in practice, helping leaders discover new ways to achieve dynamic group sessions and endowing their work with new vigour, as well as pleasure.

Facilitating Collective Intelligence brings together a wealth of knowledge and techniques from psychodrama and Jungian and systemic analysis to inform group facilitation. Throughout the book's four parts, key inner attitudes, questions and action techniques are explored to help facilitators nourish open and flexible forms of communication within groups, stimulate collective intelligence and foster creative approaches to collective problem-solving. With the help of numerous sensitively related case studies, the book guides the reader through the process of achieving more dynamism in group work, fostering creativity, encouraging agility and developing co-construction within groups. It contains more than thirty practical reference sheets which provide an instant aid for implementing the methods and models in the book. Nève-Hanquet and Crespel's approach advocates the use of action methods, specifically the ARC model, to encourage 'out of the box' thinking and develop new paths and strategies in working with teams and organisations.

Facilitating Collective Intelligence is an invaluable and essential tool in cultivating effective group dynamics for all coaches, coach supervisors and consultants, both experienced and in training. Due to its clear and practical structure, it will also be useful for counsellors, coaching psychologists and other professionals who work with groups, as well as students and academics of coaching and coaching psychology.

Chantal Nève-Hanquet's international career in psychology has encompassed psychodrama, Jungian analysis and family therapy. During fifty years working with groups, she has significantly contributed to the spread of action methods. She is a member of several international associations, including IAGP and EFTA, and a founding member and treasurer of the Belgian-based FEPTO which promotes action methods throughout Europe.

Agathe Crespel trained as a psychologist and practitioner of action methods in Belgium and France. Over the past fifteen years she has facilitated groups in various professional settings, making extensive use of action methods for supervision, coaching and the enhancement of creativity.

The authors, both members of the Brussels-based Centre for Psychosociological Training and Intervention (CFIP), have extended their practice to Italy, France, Bulgaria, Greece, Switzerland, Sweden, Turkey and the United States through numerous congresses and workshops.

Facilitating Collective Intelligence

A Handbook for Trainers, Coaches,
Consultants and Leaders

Chantal Nève-Hanquet and Agathe Crespel

Translated by Kathleen Llanwarne

LONDON AND NEW YORK

First published 2020
by Routledge
2 Park Square, Milton Park, Abingdon, Oxon OX14 4RN

and by Routledge
52 Vanderbilt Avenue, New York, NY 10017

Routledge is an imprint of the Taylor & Francis Group, an informa business

© 2020 Chantal Nève-Hanquet and Agathe Crespel

The right of Chantal Nève-Hanquet and Agathe Crespel to be identified as authors of this work has been asserted by them in accordance with sections 77 and 78 of the Copyright, Designs and Patents Act 1988.

British Library Cataloguing-in-Publication Data
A catalogue record for this book is available from the British Library

Library of Congress Cataloging-in-Publication Data
Names: Nève-Hanquet, Chantal, author. | Crespel, Agathe, author.
Title: Facilitating collective intelligence : a handbook for trainers, coaches, consultants and leaders / Chantal Náeve-Hanquet and Agathe Crespel.
Description: Abingdon, Oxon ; New York, NY : Routledge, 2019. | Includes bibliographical references and index.
Identifiers: LCCN 2019015406 (print) | LCCN 2019017298 (ebook) | ISBN 9780429264504 (Master eBook) | ISBN 9780429555053 (Adobe Reader) | ISBN 9780429563997 (Mobipocket) | ISBN 9780429559525 (ePub) | ISBN 9780367209667 (hardback) | ISBN 9780367209674 (pbk.)
Subjects: LCSH: Group facilitation. | Swarm intelligence. | Small groups.
Classification: LCC HM751 (ebook) | LCC HM751 .N48 2019 (print) | DDC 302.2—dc23
LC record available at https://lccn.loc.gov/2019015406

ISBN: 978-0-367-20966-7 (hbk)
ISBN: 978-0-367-20967-4 (pbk)
ISBN: 978-0-429-26450-4 (ebk)

Typeset in Optima
by Apex CoVantage, LLC

To Kathleen, our translator: you entered into our approach through the doors of your own lived experience and found ways of *deepening the connections* that came to light; you employed the *art of questioning* to prompt clarification of our ideas and how they were given shape in our book; you found your own path to *adopting* our approach and, through your finely tuned exercise of the art of translation, viewed our text *from a new angle* and endowed the book with new life. Your work is akin to the ARC procedure here proposed: to expand, through experience shared with others, the field of our representations, and to move, on this basis, along a path that will lead to change.

Thank you.

If you want to obtain unprecedented results, try using unprecedented methods.

Peter Senge

Contents

Foreword

In the summer of 2018, I attended an international congress in Malmö, Sweden. Walking up some steps on my way to the next workshop, I noticed Chantal Nève-Hanquet above me on the staircase, heading in the same direction. I called out to her enthusiastically. Chantal stopped, turned around, extended her hand towards me, and exclaimed, 'Ah, Daniela, come here, I have something important for you . . .'.

What Chantal handed to me was a letter from her close colleague and friend Pierre Fontaine, a Belgian pioneer in re-introducing into Europe the action methods founded by Jacob L. Moreno. Chantal and Pierre, with their long and acclaimed international career, had together been the trainers who first introduced me to the action methods that would come to be such a defining feature of my own personal, professional and social identity.

At the core of Moreno's philosophy, we encounter the notions of *Present* and *Moment*. While the present is, by definition, a transition of the past to the future, Moreno explains that, through a spontaneous-creative process, the *Present* attains dynamic meaning when it turns into a *Moment*. Seen in this way, Chantal Nève-Hanquet has always appeared, in the 'present' of my life, as a special 'moment', in a truly influential way!

I first met Agathe in person during the same international event. I learned that Chantal's masterful skills and expertise in fostering transformation within groups and teams of professionals had been recognized and deeply admired by her younger colleague; that Agathe, over many years, had been asking questions, discussing Chantal's answers and writing them down, thereby consolidating, step by step, her own familiarity with action methods as practiced in professional contexts; and above all that, as Agathe recounted, Chantal never ceased emphasizing the importance of exercising creativity 'at any and every moment'.

I learned also that, in 2014 after several years of such 'co-creation', Agathe had proposed that the two of them should organise all this invaluable knowledge into book form. During the ensuing years, therefore, the authors continued the dialog, spending much time together in each other's homes – working on their project as they cooked, washed up, or ironed – or speaking on the phone, working also while travelling, together or separately, to facilitate groups in various forms of professional setting or to attend their own professional gatherings.

Both Chantal and Agathe are principally based at the Centre for Psychosociological Training and Intervention (CFIP) in Belgium. At the same time, through membership of various international professional associations and organisations, they have extended and disseminated their practice to numerous countries including Bulgaria, Canada, France, Greece, Italy, Sweden, Switzerland, Turkey and the United States, thereby building up an increasingly international network.

Chantal and Agathe's book offers readers practical tools for exploring the potential of action methods and applying them in a wide range of organisational settings as a means of enlivening the working environment and enhancing connectedness in the workplace as well as in other types of social group context. The book's intended audience is, as indicated by its title, trainers, coaches, consultants and leaders; and its unique feature may be said to lie in its invitation to communicate through sensitivity, to recognize the 'inner disposition' or specific nature of any group, insofar as this is the dimension most likely to assist any facilitator in understanding and supporting the participants *qua* group. This sensitive and careful approach, aimed in the first instance at the creation of a safe space within which to foster the development and exercise of collective intelligence, will help any and every facilitator – trainer, coach, consultant, leader, supervisor, teacher, coordinator, politician, mediator, human resources professional – to achieve genuinely effective group work.

Users of this handbook will find in it the tools they need to propose to the teams with whom they are working a wide range of experimental exercises and experiences offering the potential to transform the experience of work – above all of 'working together' – by stimulating group members to envisage new perspectives and come up with fresh solutions. The book consists of four parts, including thirty-three 'reference sheets' and numerous wide-ranging examples for easy and effective application.

To return now to Jacob L. Moreno's concept of the *Moment*, we might say that this book was created from three important *Moments*, constitutive of a process. The first seeds were planted by Chantal Nève-Hanquet in the form of her rich professional experience; and so a plant grew, gently nurtured by Agathe and everyone else involved; and this growth produced a beautiful flower in the form of a unique and valuable tool that will generate new seeds among its readers destined to continue, propagate and enhance the forms of group process required if organisations are to contribute to the flourishing of humanity.

Today, exactly as in my memory from the summer of 2018, Chantal is standing on the stairs and has extended her hand towards the future readers, warmly exclaiming, 'Ah, everyone, come here . . . I have something important for you . . .'. And Agathe is standing, with her beautiful smile, right next to her, extending her hand as well . . . .

They have successfully co-created their long dreamed-of book and are offering the gift of it to all of us.

Daniela Simmons, PhD

Board Certified Trainer, Educator,
Practitioner (TEP) in Psychodrama,
Sociometry and Group Psychotherapy

Vice President, American Society of
Group Psychotherapy and
Psychodrama (ASGPP), www.asgpp.org

Executive Editor, The Journal of Psychodrama,
Sociometry, and Group Psychotherapy,
http://asgppjournal.org/

Director, Expressive
Therapies Training Institute (ETTi)

www.ettinstitute.com

Credit Lines

All images have been used with permission of © Baudouin Deville

Introduction

Facilitating collective intelligence

Agility relates to the inner capacity of persons and groups to develop their own ways of moving forward

The role of a facilitator is to ensure that the process of collective intelligence within the group is, indeed, as the name suggests, 'made easier'.

In a wide range of professional contexts, people are asking questions, moving forward, and seeking to develop original approaches that will enable them to work in new and more effective ways:

- *I work in an office and would like to suggest to my colleagues some techniques that would help make our meetings more lively and effective.*

- *I am a teacher and am developing methods designed to make my classes more alive.*

- *I am a manager and want to propose a context for teamwork that would encourage innovation.*

- *I am a coach and am developing ways of working that involve the body.*

- *I am a coordinator developing a project for which I would like to secure the full involvement of my team.*

- *I am involved in group supervision and am keen to broaden my range of tools for effective intervention.*

It is beneficial to stimulate the collective intelligence of a group in order to help it develop a project, come up with new initiatives and strategies for action, innovate, create, extricate itself from a difficult situation, embrace change, organise a brainstorming session, clarify roles, identify needs, take decisions, improve communication, or develop new ways of thinking and seeing. In all such contexts, to facilitate collective intelligence is to enable participants to find their own answers to the many forms of question arising.

A collective intelligence context is a kind of synchronisation, a form of osmosis that emerges within a group. Something happens that enables a situation to 'gel'. Analogies would be a successful jazz improvisation, people together breaking into song, a spontaneous dance formation, or instances of how synchronisation among team sports players sets in motion a particular 'frequency' or 'vibration'. Such synchronisation among persons can give rise to a collective experience and a joint creation representing a potential of a quite different order than the sum of the individuals forming the group.

It is difficult to put into words exactly what it is that enables this synergy. Yet we do know that dimensions associated with ways of being, inner attitude, or context, as well as with the culture and history of persons, groups and organisations, play a significant role in this respect.

It sometimes happens that attempts to implement change organised by high-level professionals run aground because they fail to take sufficient account of key persons involved, of aspects of their context, culture and history. In a project that seemed to have been well thought out in advance, developments thus fail to go as intended.

Difficulties of this kind can give rise to a sense of inertia, to an impression that things have become so stuck that the situation seems impossible to handle, as if people had lost their ability to think creatively and that there is no way of moving forward.

The manner in which a facilitator creates a safe context and accompanies a team can help participants to develop a spirit of resilience, the ability to bounce back out of difficult situations, to move on after a difficult experience, to find meaning in what is happening, and to restore the ability to think and move forward together.

Three channels of inspiration

This book, first published in 2018 by the French publisher Eyrolles, proposes approaches developed from the experience of Chantal Nève-Hanquet, having its roots in three principal sources of reference, initially developed essentially in the therapeutic arena:

- Inspiration provided by the philosophical and psychological writings and practice of Carl Gustav Jung.
- The systemic analysis approach, particularly as developed in the area of family therapy and human resources in the workplace.
- The psychodrama movement created by Jacob Levy and Zerka Toeman Moreno.

Having proved their value in the clinical field, all three approaches also have a great deal to contribute in several areas of human affairs, including the daily professional lives of men and women. Organisations and work teams can gain additional 'fulfilment' and greater success in their projects from constructive approaches based on insights developed in these fields.

The approach developed by Carl Gustav Jung (1875–1961) discloses ways of gaining contact with the deeper 'self' and with processes whereby human beings are enabled to achieve their full potential and to experience a form of wholeness. Jung's philosophy invites us to find meaning in coincidence and to focus our attention on the present moment. This Jungian input is of particular relevance in Part 1 of the book.

> Through this book, the facilitator will be invited by Carl Gustav Jung to 'discard nothing', by the proponents of systemic analysis to 'view everything in its context' and by the psychodramatists to accompany groups in learning to 'see the world through new eyes'.

The systemic approach to the whole field of human interactions, as developed in the Palo Alto School set up by Gregory Bateson (later joined by Paul Watzlawick and many others) in the early 1950s, refers to the importance of recontextualising human experience. In this process, it stresses the need to establish positive connotations, to focus on the role played by implicit rules and to consider the function of each element or event within an overall system. These systemic insights have influenced, in particular, Part 2 of the book.

The novelty of the psychodrama method initially devised by Jacob Levy Moreno (1889–1974) and his wife Zerka Toeman Moreno (1917–2016) is that the body is brought into play as an approach to fostering change. This method entails techniques whereby individuals and groups can, through embodied experience, allow themselves to be *surprised* by roles or ways of being that they discover within themselves. Part 3 of this book presents five action techniques inspired by psychodrama.

Technique aside, the reader will discover an approach to facilitation imbued with sensitivity to the whole sphere of human relations, together with references that may help to answer an unusual question that is well worth exploring in depth: *What is it that enables a group to become more alive?*

Every facilitator can take up and make use of these clues and insights, in the context of his or her theoretical references, training, and preferred methodological approaches, and while retaining his or her personal comfort zone, style, preparedness to take risks, understanding, and touch.

Which part(s) of the book should you consult?

Part 1: Key inner attitudes that will facilitate communication

> The role of facilitator is that of group musician or 'leader of the band': it is a question, then, of knowing how to tune one's instrument.
>
> *For facilitators seeking to improve their professional competence and skills through a personal effort to adjust their own mindset and attitudes. For those who wish to become more open in their approach to communicating with groups.*

Part 2: Key questions to activate collective intelligence

To be a facilitator is to be in possession of several keys that can help the group to form an effective unit and to move in the direction of its goals.

For facilitators whose dream is to create spaces that encourage innovation, creativity and the emergence of collective intelligence.

Part 3: Five key action techniques for broadening the field of possibilities

To act as facilitator is to be familiar with techniques designed to enable people to find answers to their questions.

For facilitators whose ambition is to mobilise groups to regard any given situation from several angles.

Parts 1 and 2 of this book represent a prerequisite for building a safe frame and deriving benefits from the action techniques.

Part 4: Thirty-three reference sheets for group facilitation

To be a facilitator is to become fully immersed in the meeting with a group.

For facilitators who wish, at a glance, to recall the aids and clues offered in this book and to use them for inspiration as levers for their work before, during and after facilitation sessions.

The reference sheets are classified in alphabetical order.

Readers will find explanations of specialised terms in the glossary at the end of the book.

Key inner attitudes to facilitate communication

An openness combined with a developed inner sense of the other person's reality is required in every professional situation that entails work with others in pursuit of a common aim

What kind of context will foster osmosis within the group, favouring an alchemy in which the group takes on an identity of its own such that it becomes more than the sum of the individuals forming it? What is it that enables one group to 'gel' while another does not? How can we work towards an inner process of openness to others, of a sense of the collective, of empathy, of solidarity in professional contexts where such qualities will enable the group to be imbued with a special kind of purpose and strength?

The approach via the neurosciences – and, specifically, some of the recent research considering the applicability of 'mirror-neuron' findings to the human brain and psyche – enables us to become even more aware that empathy, as well as being a psychological and deeply human disposition, is also a capability directly linked to our brain and one which, like all skills, can be stimulated and learned.

What some recent scientific research may seem to suggest is that neurological processes enable us to connect information in the realm of the senses, emotions and intellect, and thus to capture 'something' of another person's intention and emotion. The mirror neurons may thus enable us to put ourselves 'in another's place'. Unleashed by, among other things, the other person's emotions, they are sometimes referred to as 'empathy neurons'; and so it comes to seem that emotion may perhaps literally be labelled 'contagious'. The developing field of neuropedagogy stresses the importance of stimulating children's emotions and sensitivity as well as cognition and bodily movement.

Mimicking, or the act of imitating someone else, is not merely a formal – or 'surface' – imitation; it connects with the inner life of another person, with that person's intentions, representations, emotions and desires. It may therefore be thanks to the mirror neurons that we can improve our ability to fine-tune our emotional and cognitive capacities, enabling us to identify the desires and intentions of the other, to understand this other person better, and to enter into relation with him or her.

To understand the other person, with all the implications in terms of psychological and neurological disposition, is to broaden one's individual and one-sided point of view and to think more broadly.

> A group's capacity to co-create is dependent on participants' ability and preparedness to demonstrate an inner sense of another person's reality. Such 'empathy' may be considered in the light of, among many other things, the discovery of mirror neurons first reported in 1995 by Giacomo Rizzolatti and his team.

> Through experiments designed to foster our empathy, our brains are physiologically linked up with one another and thus, in the words of Jean Michel Oughourlian, they operate in Wi-Fi and Bluetooth mode!

Training for communication – the different forms of coaching, supervision, mediation and group facilitation – could refer more widely and specifically to the findings of the neurosciences, taking account of the importance of stimulating emotion and sensitivity together with cognition and bodily movement in order to create contexts that would stimulate empathy and understanding of the other.

Setting up a safe frame and stimulating cohesion within the group is a first route into fostering empathy. Simultaneously, the facilitator's inner stance, the fact that s/he has devoted time and effort to developing a sensitively attuned personal mindset and way of being, will have effects on the group.

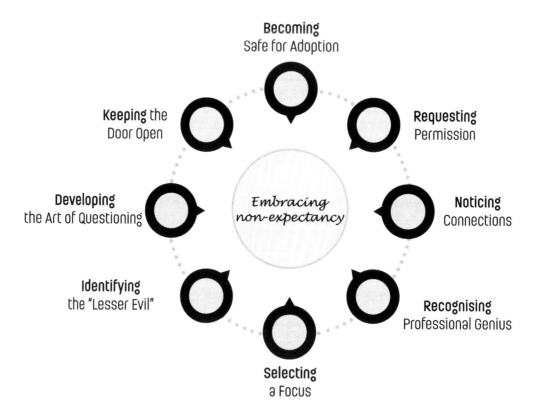

Figure 1 Nine key inner attitudes to facilitate communication

What inner stance or attitudes can I seek to adopt and develop?

A particular philosophy of life, or inner disposition, and the associated approaches chosen for engaging with the group will foster within oneself and in the group context new forms of presence to oneself and others. And this reflective approach – an inner stance on which it can be hard to pin a label – represents a necessary and important step in fostering collective intelligence.

The inner attitudes described next may inspire facilitators to develop new ways of engaging with the group while in each case respecting a facilitator's personal style.

Attitude 1: becoming 'safe for adoption'

Opening up space in oneself and inviting the other to step forward

> Adopting a 'one-down position', becoming sensitive to the other person's characteristics, resources, and skills, lending oneself to 'adoption', are ways of enabling co-construction, of incorporating resources contributed by all persons present. *How can I become 'safe for adoption'?*

To become 'safe for adoption' within a group setting is, for a facilitator, to show sensitivity to participants' resources and characteristics and to seek ways of making oneself 'adoptable'. Adjustment of one's own stance along these lines will foster relationship in the manner in which an adoptive parent seeks to become 'adoptable' by the child, enabling *this* child to find closeness – including physical closeness – to *this* adoptive parent. For such closeness to become a reality requires a holistic approach, entailing much inner work in the realms of the psyche, the emotions, and the body.

The whole art of the facilitator is to adjust to the group in this way, thereby enabling *this* group and its members to 'adopt' *this* facilitator in the context of the topic or set of issues that they have come together to explore.

> What takes place in the meeting with a group is something akin to a reciprocal 'adoption'.

In a group setting, one way of becoming adoptable may be, for example, to focus on the abilities and specific skills of those present. The facilitator takes up a position – of the body and of the psyche – that signifies: 'I am here to encourage and to foster a meeting, to receive what you are bringing to our gathering today'. The facilitator's 'adoptability' will thus find expression through a welcoming stance and gestures: a physical posture, tone of voice, look, and manner of addressing the group.

There may be times when a facilitator takes herself in hand, momentarily placing her personal expectations or demands on hold, deciding to withhold a comment that she had thought essential. This attitude sometimes helps the group to move closer to her stance.

In this way, each facilitator can, while retaining his or her own style, seek a way of becoming more adoptable, taking account of the other, opening up a space for the other to inhabit.

Attitude 2: requesting permission

And if a person says 'yes', it means that a space has opened up

> When we are about to ask people to open their minds to new situations or experiences and we first enquire whether they are prepared to do this, we allow each the opportunity to state where s/he stands.
>
> *Do I have your permission to propose a new experiment to you?*

How?

The request for permission is an invitation to open up. It is a way of allowing each group member to say where he or she stands and to create a climate of explicit endorsement. It is a way of 'knocking before entering', of asking whether or not it is permissible to burst the bubble of the individual person or the group.

It may also be a precaution taken, before addressing persons and groups, with a view to respecting their own pace and rhythm. 'Do you think you might agree to share here some aspects of professional situations that you find problematic?' or 'Do you think that, at this stage, you might consent to modify your usual way of operating in a team?'

In requesting permission from persons and from groups, a facilitator pauses to draw attention to the fact that 'something is going to happen', that change is in the air. He may, for example, address the participants by saying:

> – *Could you, at this stage, consent to share the difficulties that you experience in your team?*

To ask for permission is to invite groups to become receptive and prepared to contribute to building progress together with others.

The request for permission can be very useful in joint facilitation situations where two facilitators are working in tandem. It then becomes a flexible way of putting forward suggestions for procedure, while showing respect for the co-facilitator's leadership.

These adjustments can be made out loud, in front of the group, which also has much to learn from such exchanges:

> – *Would you, as co-facilitator, agree if I were to propose to the group an action technique to tackle the issue that has arisen?*
>
> – *Yes, why not, but let's perhaps wait until after the break.*
>
> – *Of course.*

In this way it is possible to let the co-facilitator know that one is ready to help and accede to his wishes in a context of co-construction.

Attitude 3: noticing connections

What connections exist between you and me?

To be constantly attentive to the notion of connection, to set out from the conviction that all things are interlinked and dependent on each other, is to feed a living process. Working on what connects people to one another is to foster cohesion and co-construction.

What is it that connects you?

How?

The factor connecting people in a group is something that takes place in the interactive field and therefore belongs neither to one person present nor to another. It is built up mutually, co-constructed by those present.

Connections between the members of a group are transmitted by dimensions linked to spoken language as well as by others associated with non-verbal language. When a facilitator has developed a sensitivity to these factors of interconnection within a group or team and is able to put a name to them, this serves to increase cohesion. The experience of persons present then transcends the individual dimension.

Information can sometimes be communicated in a manner that remains unspoken. In such cases people discover that, by chance, they share connections of which they were previously unaware. In group

Identifying factors of connection is a way of allowing people to meet one another through channels that discard all forms of judgement.

work, when individuals choose one another for work in sub-groups, 'coincidences' of this kind sometimes become apparent.

Jean chose Karl to work with her on a project. It turned out that Karl, by chance, had previously worked on a similar project with one of his previous employers. Yet Jean, in choosing to work with Karl, had not been in possession of this specific piece of information. In this case the connection, the link between the two individuals, was established at a level other than that of conscious and rational communication.

Sensitivity to similarities that emerge in this way is a means of broadening the interrelatedness of all that goes on. A chance occurrence, a sound, a colour, a person entering or leaving the room, any such factor or incident can be read as being linked in some way to whatever topic the group is currently working on.

This is an aspect that corresponds closely to Jung's emphasis on the phenomenon and importance of synchronicity. Influenced by Chinese thought, and particularly the book of Chinese wisdom, the *I Ching*, this approach seeks to draw attention to the fact that nothing happens by chance. In his foreword to the *I Ching*, Jung wrote: 'The irrational fullness of life has taught me never to discard anything'.

> The facilitator thus sets out from the assumption that nothing is purely fortuitous, that numerous 'happy coincidences' do indeed take place.

Unexpected happenings or findings are perceived as having some connection with what is currently going on within the group: 'What connection can we find between the power-cut that has lasted for over five minutes and our thoughts here within the team about how we are going to distribute the roles?'

Attitude 4: recognising 'professional genius'

I see the genius in you!

> Observation and work on the inner self can enable discovery of unprecedented and creative ways of moving forward in relationship with another person. The 'genius of the professional' lies in finding ways to relate and communicate in situations that seemed hopelessly blocked and in enabling the other person's skills and personal competences to come into their own.
>
> *How can I develop my sensitivity to skills and capacities that are already present?*

How?

Cultivating the 'genius of the professional' is cultivating the assumption that each person and each group has a specific form of competence. When a facilitator starts out from this hypothesis, she possesses the 'genius' for noticing and paying attention to 'small miracles'.

> Discovering the 'genius of the professional' requires an inner disposition attuned to all that is alive and constructive, within oneself, in the other, in the group, as well as inside an organisation.

It is, for example, allowing oneself to be surprised by a constructive attitude on the part of a participant whose comments or behaviour might previously have seemed little to the point. It is to pick up on that constructive attitude, and bring it to the group's attention. When a facilitator names the forms of 'genius' present in individuals or in the group, he stimulates the living springs of collective intelligence.

Attitude 5: selecting a focus

Enlivening our choices

> In making a choice, we stake out a path. The chooser takes on the role of actor. Every choice entails renunciation, affirmation, the acceptance of boundaries. How do we renounce some possibilities and espouse others while remaining within a dynamic of participation and co-construction? A choice guided by a decision to privilege one aspect in particular will prove life-affirming and will set in motion a constructive dynamic.
> *On what aspect do I choose to focus?*

How?

A facilitator who has learned to espouse the aspect on which s/he has chosen to focus will remain on the move and will naturally generate a dynamic in line with this choice.

When a facilitator is explicit about the aspect on which he has chosen to focus, he brings to the fore this notion of choice:

> The act of attending to and keeping mind and body attuned to a privileged focus will endow this aspect with a more powerful reality than the alternatives that have been set aside.

- *I've chosen to focus on this task rather than that one.*

- *I've chosen to use this working method rather than that one.*

- *I've chosen to use the time available to move forward with our stipulated task rather than as 'listening time'.*

This whole question of 'choices to be made' is just as important for individuals as it is for work teams and organisations. In some contexts, the facilitator may ask individual participants to state their own chosen focus.

Attitude 6: identifying the 'lesser evil'

Finding room for manoeuvre in the most restrictive situation

> In searching for the *best* solution, one can sometimes become discouraged in advance. To guide one's research by 'small steps' forward and motivated by the notion of 'lesser evils' is one way of opening up space for progress. Allowance can then be made for mistakes and compromise, encouraging a dynamic based on experimentation rather than perfectionism. Asking this question, in relation to oneself as well as to others, is a way of broadening the field of possibilities.
> *Which of the possible solutions represents the lesser evil?*

How?

If we insist on seeking the 'right solution', a situation can seem completely blocked. Every facilitator has experienced this feeling of powerlessness within himself as well as among the group. This is the right moment at which to seek the 'lesser evil'. Asking someone to find the *right* solution is to make an excessive demand. But the question, 'what might be the lesser evil?', is more likely to prompt the other person to effect the inner shift required to envisage the whole situation differently and thereby come up with new ideas.

> The more one works on the 'small', the greater are the chances that something will happen.

People frequently set themselves idealistic objectives. Choosing the 'lesser evil' is to start out from the assumption that there *are* no *good* solutions. It is therefore to open up a space, sometimes very small and yet frequently nonetheless sufficient for the situation to 'bounce back'. In highly complex professional situations, where room for manoeuvre is minimal, it can therefore be easier and less stressful to think about what might represent the lesser evil.

This work on assessing what might be the 'lesser evil' has frequently been of help to people faced with constraints that had seemed insurmountable.

Attitude 7: developing the art of questioning

A question asked is a problem half solved

> The art of questioning is to develop an attitude that enquires rather than affirms.
> *What makes you think that . . .?*

How?

The art of questioning is a way of setting representations in motion and beginning to view the situation from a different angle. Open questions invite the other to supply relevant information and offer the opportunity to acknowledge the complexity of every situation.

– *In what ways is it important for you that . . .?*

– *What is it that makes such-and-such the case?*

– *What makes you think that . . .?*

– *What do you mean by that?*

– *In relation to what has just been said, what strikes you in particular?*

– *In the wake of what has just been shared, what would you like to say?*

– *In the context of your reasons for attending this gathering, what are the areas that you would like to consider in greater depth so as to move forward?*

– *What has particularly struck you about what has just happened, and in relation to which points would you like to describe your responses to the group?*

Circular questions will activate a process that can alter how the persons questioned see things. This process may be fostered by introducing an absent third party into the situation. One of several types of circular question involves bringing one person to step into the shoes of another:

> By asking open questions the facilitator opens up a space into which to receive the complexity of each situation.

– *How would our client, if he were sitting here with us at this table, explain our way of working?*

– *What do you think a visitor might say if he were to discover our ways of working for the first time?*

– *How would our founder explain the changes in the mission of our organisation?*

– *How might our clients define this new project that we are seeking to develop?*

> Circular questions are particularly useful for opening up the field of representations and extending the frontiers of thought.

By means of this indirect way of eliciting information or 'circularising' the question, one creates information and enables other participants to create more information.

Attitude 8: embracing non-expectancy

Non-expectancy lies at the centre of the attitudes

To set aside expectations is to open up to the possibility of accepting loss and experiencing moments of 'bereavement'. Embracing non-expectancy lets in the possibility of surprise, whether through the situation, the other, or oneself. It allows a new dimension to emerge. In a state of non-expectancy, by displacing immediate desires in favour of deeper contact with the self, it is possible also to experience a sense of fullness.

What is it that I am being asked to give up in order to move forward?

How?

On the final page of his autobiography, Carl Gustav Jung wrote, summing up his life, 'Nothing but unexpected things kept happening to me'. Indeed, it is often when we are least expecting them that things happen.

When a situation is not proceeding as we would wish, we are bound to feel some disappointment. The attitude of non-expectancy may be understood as a laboratory of creative resilience, a preparedness to set aside earlier hopes or preferences and to enter a state of receptiveness in relation to the present moment.

It is thus that non-expectancy connects with the other attitudes to which it lends dynamism, making them more alive. Non-expectancy brings with it not only the possibility of letting go but also of allowing oneself to be surprised. A facilitator places himself in a space that is mid-way between non-expectancy and the pursuit of his aims, in a state of tension that allows new elements to appear.

> Allowing the group to set to work and be surprised at what emerges is, paradoxically, a stance of non-expectancy that allows new elements to come to light.

When a facilitator takes up a position in non-expectancy, her location is no longer that of her own wishes in relation to a person or a group. It then frequently happens that she will be surprised by what the group comes up with by way of a new opening, and this is a form of creativity that may well be accompanied by something resembling pleasure.

The expression does not refer to quite the same experience as what we speak of as 'letting go'. Sometimes, if we say to a person 'it is time to let go', we may be asking too much. The expression 'letting go' entails constraint; one is expected to give up something that one owns or has already acquired. The notion of 'non-expectancy' refers rather to a deliberate inner shift towards a position within the self that is devoid of expectation.

When a training session is about to take place, though there may well exist a set of general aims, the facilitator does not know what is going to take shape and, in this sense, the session will become the work of the participants present. To choose, when accompanying a group, to facilitate the circulation of free speech means placing one's trust in whatever is about to be born. It is to believe in the power of the group and to open oneself up to surprises. Such an attitude entails absolute trust in whatever may be about to happen.

> When we speak of 'non-expectancy', we are talking about living in the present moment and seeing what happens. In inhabiting the present moment in this way, it is possible that something unexpected may come about and it is at such a moment that a new opening can emerge.

Attitude 9: keeping the door open

What else would you like to add?

> Through a process of interiorisation, every facilitator will have developed inner attitudes of his/her own that are an invaluable tool in his/her personal approach to life and way of working.
> *What existential stance is most essential to me in my own life and work?*

This ninth attitude, the attitude of openness, might have been represented by a simple question mark. Its purpose is to leave each facilitator free to add – to all that has been proposed earlier – whatever other inner attitudes make sense to him or her. It is important that each facilitator should respect his own style, her own creativity, an individual comfort zone, and thus develop within her/himself singular attitudes that encourage new openings to emerge.

Taking it further

As explained on Reference sheet 15, it is possible also to compile a set of cards with the nine attitudes and to use this for inner work on the self. Participants might be asked, for example, to draw an 'attitude card' face down from the pack and then consider what meaning it holds for them. It is worth pointing out that the act of 'drawing a card from the pack' is a form of 'action technique' because it 'makes something happen'; it is a question of 'seizing the moment', and the work being undertaken receives its impetus from chance. Attention is thus drawn to the here and now, for chance endows with meaning the work being done at this precise moment in time.

When, after a group working session in which the attitude dimension has been stimulated, the facilitator invites individuals to draw an attitude card and see what sense they can make of it, something about the attitude in question has frequently already been internalised and the participants are familiar with an experience to which they will be able to give a name on the basis of the particular card they draw.

A few illustrations of what a facilitator might say:

- Becoming 'safe for adoption'
  - *You are the ones familiar with your area of work, so I will need you to help me if I am to help you.*
  - *In this new job, how are you going to make yourself safe for adoption? How are you going to adjust to and soak up this new environment?*

- Requesting permission
  - *Will you allow me to propose to you a working experiment that is slightly different from what we have been doing so far?*

- Noticing connections
  - *I'm going to ask you to split up into smaller groups and to talk together about connections you discover among members of your sub-group?*
  - *What I have noticed is that there are several factors of connection among you. For example, several of you have spoken of the importance of respect and communication within the team.*

- Recognising 'professional genius'
  - *What you've just said is extremely interesting and it enables us to move forward.*
  - *You have found a solution to the problem, thanks to your particular expertise in this field, and that is precisely what we mean by the 'genius of the professional'!*

- Selecting a focus
  - *In spite of all the emotion circulating here in the room and ideas shooting out in so many directions, we will stop this exchange here. We will choose to give priority to the decision taken this morning to take a break at noon. And so we will continue after the break. Since there isn't going to be time to finish everything, on what will you choose to focus?*

- Identifying the lesser evil
  - *In this complex situation that you are experiencing, what do you think would represent the lesser evil?*

- Developing the art of questioning
  - *Where are you up to at this precise moment?*

- *How might you communicate, using questions rather than assertions, with this person who is so reluctant to change?*

● Embracing non-expectancy

- *What do you risk losing if you stop here and what are you likely to gain? Can you bring yourself to live with things however they may turn out?*

- *You say that you want to leave this group immediately and not come back. Do you think you might agree to stay until the end of the day and see what happens? And then, when today is over, you could decide whether to stay or whether you still wish to leave the group.*

- *In this context, given the pressure you are under, what would it mean, here at this moment, to be in a state of non-expectancy?*

● Keeping the door open

- *If you were to connect with an inner attitude that is both familiar and important to you, what would that be?*

Authors in conversation

Agathe: I've noticed that certain phrases recur frequently, like leitmotifs, in your manner of addressing persons and groups. These are a living dimension of the way you intervene. You refer to non-expectancy, co-construction, adoptability, trusting the process taking place in the group, and so on.

Chantal: There do exist inner attitudes that can encourage flexibility, open-mindedness, the ability to bounce back, the emergence of new resources, an ability to open up and see things differently. It is a question of making oneself available, 'adoptable', in a manner that enables the group to take ownership of the work being done. In this way they will move forward in this space of the here and now.

Agathe: You speak about grief and losses suffered on a daily basis and you also refer to 'non-expectancy'. What is the reason for this?

Chantal: To embrace a state of non-expectancy is to be prepared to experience a kind of grief and to ask a question along the lines of 'what is it that I am being asked to give up in order to move forward?' It is admitting to oneself that this is an experience akin to renunciation. If, at a certain moment, I choose to listen in silence when someone is saying something, it can be an experience of renunciation, especially if the point I had wished to make was an idea to which I was particularly attached. It is a question in such cases of managing to retain contact with my own self but in a way that is different from expressing my own point of view which earlier seemed to me like the best way forward . . . .

Agathe: Often you begin the group work with exercises that help participants to connect with one another.

Chantal: Let me tell you about an experience that marked me. At one time I regularly had the opportunity to offer hitchhikers long-distance lifts in my car. One day, on the spur of the moment, I asked one of them, 'What do you think you and I might have in common?' This was a pretty surprising outburst, but we began to search for connections between us and our exchange enabled me to realize that we really did have a lot in common, both personally and professionally. From that day on I have been devising experiments to enable people to explore what they have in common with others. It is one way of creating a context of empathy.

Agathe: What exactly do you have in mind when you speak about the 'genius' of professionals'?

Chantal: Let me tell you another story. A few years ago, also while driving, I was listening to a radio programme in which I heard an interview about *The Diving Bell and the Butterfly*, a book whose author, Jean-Dominique Bauby, was afflicted with locked-in syndrome: he was completely paralysed, yet conscious. A visitor, noticing that his friend did have the movement of his left eyelid, realized that this could perhaps represent a way of enabling the paralysed man to communicate. And so he had the brilliant idea of showing him letters of the alphabet and asking him to move his eyelid in response to specific letters, for the purpose of creating words. The idea proved fruitful. The paralysed man had found a means of expression. In this way Jean-Dominique Bauby was able to 'write' a book about his experience in the wake of his accident.

Thanks to the brilliant observation of a person who knew him well, this man was able to tell his story. 'That is a form of genius', I said to myself. Since then I have always been careful to draw attention, by naming them, to instances of 'genius' in persons and groups that I meet.

Summary Part 1

Creation of a context that fosters *empathy* is an indispensable ingredient in the emergence of collective intelligence. The neurosciences have shown us that empathy is a disposition, simultaneously psychological and neurological, that lends itself to stimulation.

Some specific modes of communication with groups represent an invitation to enter a particular state of mind, a way of being, a form of openness, flexibility and agility in relation to oneself, others, and every aspect of life. In this chapter, nine inner attitudes were proposed as ways of attuning oneself to the situation:

- Becoming 'safe for adoption'.
- Requesting permission.
- Noticing connections.
- Recognising 'professional genius'.
- Selecting a focus.
- Identifying the 'lesser evil'.
- Developing the 'art of questioning'.
- Embracing non-expectancy.
- Keeping the door open.

PART

2

Key questions to activate collective intelligence

Key 1: how am I going to work with the here and now?

The here and now is a lever for moving forward

> The facilitator can foster collective intelligence by listening carefully to what is taking place in the here and now of the group.

Here and now

Deriving from the Latin preposition 'pro' which means 'forward' and the verb 'cedere – cessus' meaning 'to go', 'to walk', the word 'process' represents a forward movement. A group process is thus a naturally alive and interactive forward movement to which we can pay close attention for the purpose of achieving goals identified as desirable. Such goals may relate to learning, problem-solving, cohesion, productivity, etc.

To illustrate the notion of process, let us take the example of soil. The quality of the soil, and the agricultural method selected, will determine the germination and growth of the seeds, as well as the nature of the resulting living product: cereal, vegetable, fruit, tree, shrub, etc.

To foster the life element within groups and teams is to stimulate skills and talents, presence, autonomy, creativity, openness, efficiency, productivity, flexibility, resilience, and other resources that promote movement in the direction of the goals to be achieved.

From the seed to the fruit, a process takes place. We can both imagine it and observe it, and yet we can also expect some surprises. What determines whether a seed germinates or not? What makes it develop in one way rather than another? Why is it that two identical seeds produce different variations?

Placing these questions in relation to groups: how is it that, in a context that appears similar, two groups or two persons will not react similarly? To some extent, these processes elude us.

The facilitator's role is to pay careful heed to the process underway. The questions to be asked include the following:

- *What is going on?*
- *How can we act to bring out what is taking place and make certain elements of information more explicit?*
- *On this basis, in which direction do we wish to move?*

Available action techniques will be selected and used in accordance with the facilitator's analysis of the process, frequently on the spur of the moment. The decision in favour of the most appropriate technique lies in the facilitator's hands. In other words, whatever the facilitator proposes will be built up – 'co-constructed' – with the here and now of developments in the group. It is rather difficult, under such circumstances, to remain faithful to a script produced in advance.

> Stick rigorously to a frame, co-construct using the here and now, take account of the goal being pursued, allow oneself to be surprised, maintain a sense of playfulness and pleasure.

The facilitator, accordingly, is at the service of what is happening in the here and now just as much as of the goal being pursued.

To accompany the process is also to link up with methodological and theoretical references. Each facilitator works with his or her own familiar references. A facilitator well acquainted with the systemic approach will be able, for example, to make connections between action techniques and the systemic grid.

Illustration

To stay or to leave?

The trainer arrives at the training centre. She has come to give a training session on time management. On arrival, in discussion with an administrative officer, it turns out that there has been a mistake and that the participants have come to attend a session on stress management. The trainer is also used to giving stress management sessions but has not brought along her customary material for this type of session. The choice is as follows: to cancel the training session and send everyone back home or to decide to work with the here and now of the situation that has arisen. The trainer chooses to stay. She begins the session as follows:

Trainer (to participants):

- *Here we are in an unexpected situation. You have come to attend a training session on stress management and I had come to give you a session on time management. We could all just decide to go home again, but the fact is that we are here. I do have the knowledge and skills to facilitate a session on stress management, even though that is not what I had prepared for today. If you agree, I would propose that we take advantage of the situation in which we find ourselves and that we see what kind of connections we can make with the topic of stress management and the stressful situations you encounter in your work. On this basis we can work on specific situations that you experience and at the same time link up with theoretical aspects.*

Participants:

- *In my job I am repeatedly confronted with a* fait accompli. *This causes me terrible stress, and it is why I enrolled for this stress management session.*

- *This situation reminds me of the permanent chaos in which I work; I never have a moment's peace, something unexpected is always coming up.*

The mental agility required to make use of whatever material is to hand, to seek out 'lesser evils', to take care to request the group's permission (see earlier sections on 'inner attitudes') can help to initiate a 'shared story' between facilitator and group, and thereby stimulate the task of embarking on a process of co-construction.

Finding out more

As well described by the philosopher François Jullien, Chinese philosophy takes account above all of context and situation, detecting therein favourable resources that can be helpful on the road to maturity. The ancient book of Chinese wisdom, the *I Ching*, epitomises this approach. It becomes possible, in other words, to foster the gradual transformation of a situation such that it becomes favourable. By analogy with this eastern philosophical approach, the facilitator's role in collective intelligence is to identify resources, accompany change, and ensure that the group process is fostered in such a way that it bears fruit.

Key 2: how can I create a safe frame and context?

The frame, like a membrane, is simultaneously stable and alive

> To hold rigorously to a process will facilitate creation of a safe space for collective intelligence. The rules of spontaneity, freedom, bring-back, discretion and punctuality will enable trust, creativity, the emergence of ideas and risk-taking.

Safety

The frame, by ensuring coherence and cohesion within the group, represents a container. A safe frame is a prerequisite for the development of an alive and open spirit within the group. The frame represents what Donald W. Winnicott (1886–1971) calls 'holding'; it is, in other words, the stable, firm environment required to carry the group psyche during the inner work demanded of its participants. An alternative metaphor for designating this

> The facilitator is a tight-rope walker who oscillates between rigorously holding to the frame while maintaining a 'one-down position' so as to accompany the movement of the group.

container, or frame, might be that of a 'skin' or 'membrane' that serves to protect the group and guarantee the place of each person within it.

Thus, the frame is much more than a 'discipline' or code of good behaviour, mark of courtesy or norm. It can evolve, become more precise, and be considered simultaneously stable and alive. It breathes.

In general terms, the notion of 'safe frame' finds embodiment through tone of voice, presence, setting of spatial boundaries, supply of clues about how the work will be carried out, pacing and paying attention to transitions, guiding, choosing certain words rather than others, setting limits, placing, selecting, reorienting, making explicit, etc.

> The frame bestows importance upon the nature of the work being done and the place of each person in the group.

The five rules given next, inspired by the work of J.L. Moreno and enriched by a Jungian approach, will contribute to the experience of 'holding', or the ability of the facilitator to 'carry a group' and put in place a safe context.

- **The rule of spontaneity (or freedom of thought):** Each participant can put forward his or her ideas and any matter or topic may be mentioned, described, represented. Everyone can, for example, ask questions, establish connections, contribute thoughts.

  Spontaneity fosters participant involvement and encourages people to take initiatives.

- **The rule of freedom:** Within certain established and unavoidable constraints, each participant has personal room for manoeuvre and a margin of freedom to accept or reject any suggestion or proposal made.

  This margin of freedom allows people to commit to a project and feel motivated to contribute to it.

- **The rule of 'bring-back':** Items of information can be brought back into the group or the team, even if they were first supplied outside the official working time. This could apply, for example, to comments made during breaks. Such information represents a contribution to the work process. Indeed, conflicts and misunderstandings frequently stem from a lack of communication. In some cases, if individuals within teams had allowed themselves to supply such information, misunderstandings could have been avoided.

  The 'bring-back' can ensure the development and enrichment of a process.

- **The rule of discretion:** this requires that what belongs to the group be kept within the group; it is a question, if necessary, of choosing and deciding together what information is to be communicated beyond the team. By analogy with the notion of professional secret, participants then take it upon themselves to discern what is confidential.

The rule of discretion establishes limits and thereby guarantees respect of the process and of all those participating.

- **The rule of punctuality** means that everything has a beginning and an end. Each phase of the work begins and ends at a certain time, this time frame being clearly announced to all. Each participant is regarded as having a place and a purpose in the constituted team or group. During working hours participants are requested to keep the rest of the group informed of any possible late arrivals or early departures.

Punctuality, based on the notions of 'beginning' and 'end', means that participants are able to internalise a frame and organise themselves, both inwardly and in terms of logistics.

Some additional advice

Given the presence of smartphones, it may be advisable to expand discretion to include guidelines on taking photos:

Facilitator:

- *In order to do my work, I need some guarantees and I would ask you not to take photos or at least, before doing so, to request the group's agreement.*

If photos are taken, they form part of the process and it is important to clarify their meaning and purpose, to specify how they may support or prove useful within the overall framework, as well as to check that every participant agrees.

These different rules or work guidelines interact and feed into one another, fostering a climate of human respect and responsibility. After all, to internalise a frame is, in some ways, to internalise a sense of what is fair, thereby enabling trust among participants. Such an approach will help each individual to forge an inner stance attuned to the nature of the work to be embarked upon, thereby enhancing the overall potential for group creativity.

The person who, in a group, feels safe and experiences the process as 'well-intentioned', will internalise this experience within his or her psyche, thereby becoming able to inspire a similar experience

> Discovering for oneself that a group is capable of building something interesting will enable internalisation of the idea that groups can be vehicles for the achievement of worthwhile experiences and results.

elsewhere in a different setting. Transference is possible. To experience a secure and enabling group experience is an aid in passing such experience on to other people in other contexts. '*Because I have had this experience here, I intend to re-enact what I have felt and learned so as to pass it on to my working team*'. In other words, the 'safe frame' is, in and of itself, a factor of change.

Whether it be a question of chairing a meeting, managing a project, teaching, passing on skills, or leading a team, the purpose of the frame is to stake out a path that will enable people to move forward in an atmosphere of trust.

Illustration

Moving from competition towards cooperation and collaboration

In the interests of efficiency, several universities had been brought together under a single administration. While they were thus, 'on paper', supposed to work together, in reality each showed a tendency to operate in isolation. Elements of competition had even become apparent. A three-day training course was thus arranged with a view to creating more forms of synergy.

The course consisted of talks by experts alternating with opportunities for exchange among staff in the presence of a facilitator. The facilitator began by staking out the safety frame, proposing that, so as to encourage interaction, participants should sit in a semi-circle without any table. In the course of the first day the facilitator observed that participants quite frequently got up to leave without warning and failed to return, subsequently realising that it was habitual for members of different teams to leave a meeting discretely whenever they had something important to attend to. The facilitator then recalled the importance of stating that one was leaving because each person had an important place in the group.

The facilitator said that the chairs of people who had left should remain in the circle, even though they were empty, because their occupants, whether present or absent, remained part of the group.

From this moment onwards, for the two remaining days of the course, the notions of presence and absence were no longer the same. People who found it necessary to leave began to explain to the group why they had to leave early or would arrive late. This new attention even seemed to increase cohesion within the group and to slow down the flow of departures and arrivals.

A year later, the course organisers explained that, following this training experience, several forms of collaboration among universities were still ongoing. Some participants had suggested to the organisers that the opportunity for similar training be renewed. According to the organisers, attention to the establishment of a safe frame had played an important role in the process. This experience had long-term effects on involvement and cooperation.

Key 3: how will I stimulate cohesion?

Alone you go faster, together we go further

> Within a group, the prompting – by a range of means – of connections between participants will be a way of freeing up energy, stimulating the notion of interdependency and creating cohesion.

Cohesion

Human development starts out with 'connection': the mother and the foetus, then the child, are intimately and physically connected. The route to differentiation is enabled by the very fact that it started out with this experience of feeling connected. By analogy with human development, when the facilitator is sensitive to helping persons to connect, either by her/himself picking up on explicit or implicit connections, or by proposing experiments that bring them about, s/he creates spaces to stimulate trust within the group setting. It is easier to tackle factors of difference or of what is specific to individuals when people have first had the opportunity to connect.

In the experiments proposed and the methodologies used at the beginning of work with a group, connection can be stimulated by suggesting that people begin to walk about, to move around the room, so that their body opens up and becomes ready to participate in whatever is going to happen next. When bodies open up in this way, it becomes possible to observe a form of vibration among people, something that circulates and that connects.

Illustration

What is it that connects us?

Facilitator:

– *I propose that you start to walk around and that you form groups of three, ensuring that you get together with people you know less well, and to talk about whatever connections there are among you, in general and in relation to the topics we are here to tackle today.*

Now that ten minutes have passed, choose together what information you would like to share with the whole group to give an idea of what you have exchanged.

Participant from one group:

> – *One connection among us is that we all have strong characters. We are sensitive to stress. It so happens that two of us have close family members in the United States. Having all this in common means that we can get along very well together.*

Participant from another group:

> – *What connects us is that we are naturally optimistic (laugh). Also the fact that we are all women. And we also appreciate good food! In addition, we all agree that the atmosphere is deteriorating and that our firm was a more pleasant place to work five years ago before the changes in the senior management.*

Finding out more

It is quite possible to set in motion large groups of a hundred or more people and to get them to work together on what connects them. In such cases, the participants come together in sub-groups of seven to twelve people and an 'ambassador' from each group gives, in one or two sentences, and using a microphone if necessary, a brief account of the connections among the members of his or her sub-group. The facilitator then proposes that those who so wish should say, in a few words and on the basis of what they have heard and observed, what, for them, connects all the persons present in the group. The question of connecting features comes to signify that people are interdependent and it fosters the cohesion required for the group to get down to work. At a subsequent stage, this initial work can be used to tackle a more important question arising within the company or workplace.

Methods of facilitation in large groups, like the World Café or the Open Forum, often start out with a warm-up session dealing with 'what connects us' which brings into play the creative potential and collective intelligence of a large group.

Key 4: what can I do to strengthen participants' sense of personal competence?

Working with 'living matter'

When the facilitator is able to perceive people's abilities – or 'competences' – especially in cases where, at a first glance, they might well have been taken as forms of 'incompetence' or some other problematic manifestation, a context is created that will be conducive to change. One way of fostering the expression of personal competence will be to encourage a process of give-and-take among participants.

Competence

The psychiatrist and systemic analyst Guy Ausloos, in the 1990s, emphasised recognition of the 'competence of families' as, in family therapy, a first step towards change. Regarding families as possessing competence in this way went against the flow in a cultural context that viewed therapy in terms of a questioning of parental attitudes.

By analogy with therapy, for a facilitator to adopt as a working hypothesis that the persons, groups, and organisations with whom s/he is working possess valuable personal competence is a first, and important, building block. On the basis of such competence, the facilitator will be able to intervene.

Illustration

Quality or fault?

A head of department explains that he has difficulty managing his team, particularly when it comes to introducing change. He describes himself as 'excessively independent', as having been always accustomed to working on his own.

The facilitator enquires whether this character trait of 'independence' has proved an asset during his career for achieving success with certain projects. In systemic terms, this question represents a way of regarding 'independence' from a different angle. The facilitator takes up the notion of independence and enquires as to how such individual characteristics, regarded as a failing, might also represent a resource for the creation of alliances with others. This line manager, when he comes to regard his 'independence' from this new angle, is enabled to perceive also its positive aspects.

Apply or question?

During a training session, the facilitator asks participants to position themselves in relation to the application of a specific theoretical model. The question is formulated as follows:

Facilitator:

– *On the basis of your own experience, in what respects would you say that this model is questionable?*

The question is worded in a way that brings to the fore the professionals' own experience and personal competences rather than the applicability of a specific model. Paradoxically, insofar as the question places the stress on competence, it promotes, at the same time, an openness towards the model proposed. Professionals are thus accorded actor status rather than being regarded as passive learners.

One key that can help the facilitator foster personal recognition of each member is the stimulation of give and take within the group.

Knowing how to grant recognition to the other generates a feeling of reliability and receiving equity, in the relationship. Reciprocity comes about when the person receiving recognition is able to return it. The practice of giving and receiving thus becomes a feature central to all relationships. Ivan Börzörményi-Nagy, founder of contextual therapy, was a psychiatrist who developed the notion of a relational ethic that invites each person to work on their own responsibility and attentiveness to aspects of give and take.

For a facilitator, attentiveness to these dimensions will ensure that a person is able to experience what she receives as fair in a manner that will increase her 'constructive legitimacy' or feeling of being valued and deserving of recognition. By contrast, if what is received is experienced as unfair, a person will experience a surge of 'destructive legitimacy' and come to feel 'disqualified', as a result of which she will seek a way of restoring a sense of personal merit. The facilitator can check to ensure that what is given to persons is experienced as appropriate and fair. Should this not be the case, the facilitator will ensure that this person can express her needs. Interventions on the part of the facilitator will thus offer support in the circulation of balanced give-and-take.

For example:

- *What message do you wish to give to the group?*
- *How do you take this message?*
- *How do you take what your colleague has just said?*
- *Come to discover what the group has given you in response to what you shared.*
- *Now that your colleagues have given you their responses, how would you review your initial question?*
- *What do you feel you have taken as a result of this work that you did for yourself, carried out on your own behalf?*
- *Do you feel that what has been given to you is appropriate? Do you think it is fair?*

The fact that the facilitator is attentive to the recognition of each person's abilities and skills and to the circulation of giving and receiving will strengthen the feeling of trust within the group.

Finding out more

The purpose of the contextual approach developed by Ivan Böszörményi-Nagy (1920–2007) is to enable consolidation of trustworthiness and fairness among partners to a relationship, above all family members, but also members of a team, or even of a network. It is an approach that incorporates contributions from both psychoanalysis and systemic analysis, while at the same time offering a new way of understanding the motivations underlying behaviour. The contextual approach lays particular focus on dialogue, while emphasising aspects, such as the 'relational ethic', give-and-take, receiving, reliability, loyalty, that are constants found in all human relations.

Key 5: how will I take account of what remains unspoken?

Out of the box!

In any group process, there are components that are visible and explicit, and, at the same time, all those unspoken and implicit aspects that constitute the submerged part of the iceberg. The work of the group facilitator is to direct attention equally to the visible and to the invisible parts of the iceberg.

Implicit

An explicit message contains numerous possibilities of implicit messages. Components that are unspoken, or implicit, will, if identified, enable new doors to be opened. Taking the analogy of the iceberg, the visible section above the water represents the explicit messages, the elements that are actually communicated, spoken out loud and thereby made somehow 'official'; the submerged part, meanwhile, contains the implicit, unspoken and sometimes unconscious messages. Yet this unspoken or implicit information is nonetheless 'active' and will not be without its effects.

Taking a job interview situation as an example, it may well be that, in addition to the formal selection criteria for the post in question, employers and job applicants will be influenced by some less conscious forms of response, by information that, while implicit, will nonetheless circulate and form links among the persons present.

Such elements could be an allusion to a shared history, a reference to some family situation, a particular expression or way of speaking, or an item of clothing prompting personal memories. Such features are indicative of how aspects that are never made fully explicit are nonetheless likely to affect the recruitment procedure.

The facilitator, in creating a context for the group work, will bear in mind this complex dimension built up by so many unspoken as well as explicit components, and will remain aware that an excessively simplified vision of the processes underway will inevitably reduce the room for manoeuvre.

> To take account of complexity is to be simultaneously aware of how much is implicit, unspoken, and yet nonetheless present in the dynamic among persons, teams and organisations.

What is more, in reading situations using a systemic grid, it will be said that systems are run through with implicit rules, with a set of processes, that repeat themselves, are alive, and which also form part of the submerged section of the iceberg or of the 'unspoken'.

These rules are implicit because they are never actually stated explicitly; they are not part of the 'official programme'. Yet there exists, at the same time, an 'unofficial programme' of which they do form part and by means of which they influence movements within systems.

In a given organisation, for example, spouses never attend staff parties or other workplace recreational activities. While no formal statement has ever been issued to that effect, it is, quite clearly, an 'unwritten rule'.

In other cases organisations become caught up in paradoxical implicit rules like, 'It's important that we create the impression that we are keen to change even though we know we actually have no intention of changing'.

Within every group rules are created without members being aware of it. Though the rules themselves may not change, once people have become aware of them, they may adopt a new approach in relation to these rules, and that is when change happens.

> A facilitator will not seek to change the implicit rules that help to govern systems. S/he will help people to become more aware of the rules and thereby to be less – or differently – influenced by them.

In conclusion, we might say that our vision of how to accompany change is often based on the visible portion of the iceberg. A facilitator fully cognisant with the systemic grid will take account of the submerged portion of the iceberg which, though invisible, remains active. Facilitating change then becomes taking account simultaneously of both the official programme and all the aspects that remain unspoken.

Illustration

When change fails to bring about change

The scapegoat phenomenon provides a good illustration of the notion of implicit rule. It is frequently to be observed within groups that, when a person whose function has been that of scapegoat moves out of the department or leaves the company, another person takes on this role. This observation might lead a facilitator to hypothesise an implicit rule along the lines that *exclusion is a prerequisite for cohesion*. Regarded in this light, the scapegoat phenomenon might be seen as a group 'symptom' and, from a systemic stand-point, *every symptom has a function*.

It can also be observed that in a group or team where one person has taken on the function of scapegoat, the other members get along well and display a degree of cohesion.

In the light of this metaphor, and following our hypothesis, one working option would be to recognise the function of the scapegoat. The question to be asked might thus be as follows: '*To what extent might exclusion, in a given organisation, be endowed with meaning?*'

Once the scapegoat phenomenon is regarded from the standpoint of competence, and the function of scapegoat is separated out from the person who takes on this role, a space for exploration is opened up in the psyche. The situation can again be regarded in its complexity, people become able to create information, and this new opening stimu-lates the search for constructive solutions and levers for change.

This manner of considering implicit rules, of starting out from the assumption that everything that happens has a function, and of seeking to ascertain what competences make a system operate as it does, releases us from a dichotomy consisting of 'good' and 'bad'.

The systemic grid helps us to read a situation creatively rather than becoming stuck in judgemental attitudes.

Implicit rules are part of what is unspoken, and it is sometimes important to give them explicit formulation, thereby setting them to work and calling them into question, so as to become extricated from situations that repeat themselves and lead to dysfunction in working life.

Finding out more

Whether change is characterised as 'imposed', 'natural', 'desired' or 'unexpected', sys-temic analysis sets out to 'create a context in which change can appear'. The change referred to in systemic analysis as 'type 1 change' takes place within a system that does not itself change. From the inside of the system, type 1 change appears logical, predict-able, somehow inevitable. Consider, for example, the way in which a person or a group may be given advice so that the more advice is received, the greater the sense of incom-petence experienced by the person or group in question, leading to even greater quanti-ties of advice being bestowed upon them.

The kind of change that is referred to as 'type 2 change' alters the system. This is change that generates real change because something changes in the context. By analogy, a fight with a monster in a dream feels like a type 1 change. To wake up and realise that it was all a dream would be a type 2 change.

Certain changes, like, for example, the one described in Part 3 of this book in relation to the Revealing Chairs (see p. 99), prompt a surprise effect. By means of the action technique, the facilitator identifies an implicit rule (which in the framework of this example could be formulated as follows: 'to succeed is to convince'). Enlightened by this hypothesis, the facilitator develops a different reading of the situation and encourages another form of change that translates into a strategy different from that of convincing. In this way, the participants develop solutions that place them in a new relationship to the implicit rule.

The answer to the question becomes an unexpected one, and the persons, coming out from inside the system, experience a sense of something like a break or discontinuity. Viewed from the outside, this type 2 change can be understood as a change of reference framework.

Once the facilitator has developed a full understanding of the difference between a type 1 and a type 2 change, s/he can pay attention to this aspect and see in what respects the interventions and methods that s/he proposes will, at some moments, be a lever prompting movement towards a certain type of change.

Key 6: how will I enable the group to see a single situation from different angles?

To see the world with new eyes

> By prompting new 'openings' and amplifying their implications, we create information that will enable us to see the same situation differently.

Opening-up

As explained by Peter Senge, systems scientist and author, people expand their capacity to create the results they truly desire by experimenting with new ways of thinking. How then can we alter our gaze so as to rise above our habitual ruts? It can be difficult to solve a problem from the same level of consciousness that created it.

To facilitate a group thus means striving to stimulate participants' mental, physical, emotional, and sensorial potential in ways that will mobilise the suppleness and the internal flexibility of the group. Through this process, people's ways of seeing the world, beliefs, representations, take on bodily expression. It is important, if these patterns are to evolve, for them to be first experienced and set in movement.

A representation – or way of seeing things – 'that evolves and changes' is an individual or group of individuals subject to a process of change and endowed with the requisite suppleness to embark on a path and move forward. A representation that becomes fixed, that no longer changes, may be the sign of a system in difficulty.

The collective intelligence generated by groups is linked with this possibility demonstrated by persons to take their distance from familiar paradigms, representations and beliefs. By representing to themselves new ways of considering their problems, challenges, questions and thought processes, people are at the same time getting in touch with new resources for moving forward.

How then can we create contexts that will stimulate this agility on the part of groups and persons? Proposals for developing these forms of expansion, amplification and inner mobility are frequently issued in the form of advice and exercises linked to 'will-power'. Beyond injunctions of the type, 'you must think more broadly', how can people be offered experiences that will enable them to perform their own inner work fruitfully?

Opening up new space through the art of questioning

Rather than seeking to convince, another manner of accompanying change can be to position oneself in an inner state of questioning and of asking open questions. 'Could you say more about how it is important for you that . . .?' Or 'what do you mean by saying that . . .?' 'Circular' – or 'third-party' – questions will have the effect of creating surprise and opening up the field of representations: 'How would your competitors react and what would they say?'

Stimulating the 'surprise effect' by picking up on the here and now

One way of creating surprise is to pick up on some improbable detail. The facilitator can observe aspects, in space and time, of body language, colours, symbolic forms, words taken out of context, non-verbal forms of expression, all sorts of small things that seem to have nothing to do with what is going on and yet which possess an eloquence all their own!

By developing a sensitivity to factors of connection, setting out from the conviction that everything is interdependent and connected, the facilitator can exercise observation skills and invite the group to make connections.

If, for example, in a group, one person says something, or initiates behaviour, quite irrelevant to the work currently underway, the facilitator might alight on this

> The facilitator can practise and learn to draw group members' attention to aspects of the here and now that will prompt their surprise.

'something', thanking the person, and incorporating this 'surprise' as an analogy able to assist the group in moving towards its purpose.

Facilitator:

– *What connection could we make between the bag that has just fallen on the floor and what it was we were saying at that precise moment?*

Such a question may seem strange, and yet seizing the moment in this way is to latch on to whatever is happening in the here and now to throw light on a question; and it is to trust that the group will be able to co-construct something and, by itself, open up new space. In this way, the colour of some item of clothing, a position in space, the sight of someone fiddling with their ear or with a piece of jewellery, may suddenly attract our gaze; and the fruit of this minute observation can prompt a surprise effect that may well reveal something essential.

When the facilitator draws the group's attention to a connection between what can be observed and what is going on in the group, however peculiar this may seem, it is not necessary, as facilitator, to have an answer oneself or to have already formulated some interpretation concerning a connection. The facilitator trusts to the group's capacity for co-creation and to the power of what is happening in the here and now.

Amplifying the representational field by setting participant in movement

The action techniques described in Part 3 of this book present concrete tools for broadening the representational field. The result of such activation, which brings into play both the body and the feelings and thought processes, is to prompt movement within persons' inner worlds. In this way, people come to see the same situation from different angles.

Illustration

What to do when an attempt to convince has the opposite effect

In the framework of the medical and social care of a family, a doctor was faced with the following problem: the youngest child, an eight-month-old baby, was suffering from respiratory problems and, in particular, recurrent bouts of bronchitis. Both parents smoked in the house. Alerted to this situation, the doctor began by offering explanations and distributing brochures about the toxic effects of tobacco and dangers associated with passive smoking. Yet he soon noticed that the parents were not receptive, and that the more he tried to convince them the more recalcitrant they became in relation to any suggestion of change. He even had the impression that the relationship he had built up with them was being damaged whenever he brought up this subject. The family's argument was as follows:

> The other children, the older ones in the family, had grown up in the same environment in which we were smoking in the house. None of them had these health problems, so the cause cannot be cigarettes, it must be something else.

Here the doctor was confronted with an extremely difficult task, perhaps the most difficult of all: to find ways of establishing communication on terrain where each person holds particularly entrenched representations and beliefs.

Doctor to the family:

- *Could you say more about the importance for you of retaining the same environment for your baby as for the children who came before him?*
- *What makes you believe that your child's ill health is attributable to other causes?*
- *Could you perhaps tell us more about what you mean when you say this?*

Circular questions, which bring in a third party, also help to see the same problem from a new angle:

Doctor to the family:

- *What would your baby say if he were able to speak?*
- *What would the older children say if they were able to offer some advice about their little brother's health?*

Still in the form of questions, the doctor can then move on to make some proposals, taking one small step at a time. In this way, he seeks to bring the family round to cooperating in a search, by observing, by elaborating hypotheses, and by trying out different ways of helping the child. At each step the doctor encourages the parents to observe the effects of the 'small changes' they could put in place.

- *What would you say about trying out just one morning without smoking and seeing how the baby is breathing by midday? And next time I see you, you could tell us what you have observed. This way we could see together how we can help your baby . . . .*

Could you choose a number between 7 and 150?

In the framework of a team supervision session, a facilitator feels that the climate of trust is sufficient to try out the following surprise:

Facilitator (to a participant)

– *I see that you have a book there in front of you. How many pages does it have?*

Participant

– *150.*

Facilitator

– *Could you perhaps choose someone from the group who will be asked to give any number between 7 and 150? Then we can see what links we find between the page in question and the situation that we are working on here together.*

Participant

– *OK. I'll ask Celia.*

Celia

– *77*

Facilitator to participant

– *Would you agree to read out a couple of sentences from page 77 of your book?*

Participant (reading from the book)

– *'He felt that this order was resented by his men who hardly welcomed the idea of being outdone by a weakling. It took them a moment to locate the bow and quiver in among the weapons that had been seized from the bandits'.*

Facilitator to group

– *Thank you. Now, working all together, what kind of connection can we make between the short passage we have just heard and the situation we are currently working on here in the group?*

Participant

– *The difficult thing in our teamwork is knowing how to share authority. There is a power imbalance that we have trouble managing and that is damaging to our project.*

Participant

– *I rather like the idea of the bow and the quiver being among the weapons seized from the bandits. In fact, we have so many competitors that we are losing our market niche and reputation. It's as if we indeed need to pinpoint what it is that constitutes our true value.*

Some techniques, such as those that will be described in Part 3 of this book, enacted in the context of a safe frame, can lead to an involvement so deep as to trigger the emergence of change. This change may well be absolutely unexpected and the resulting sense of surprise is a 'felt' much more than a 'thought' experience, especially if it is one that incorporates an emotional dimension and is linked to an experience that was of the body.

Key 7: how can I remain on a (re)searching path?

Learning as we go along

As facilitator, to place oneself within a (re)search perspective is to tell oneself that there can be no 'good' or 'bad' choice when selecting facilitation methods for use. One choice may be more relevant than another at certain stages in the process. Observation, devising of hypotheses, choice of modes of intervention and observation of the effects of this intervention will guide the facilitator's search and, on this basis, he will devise new working hypotheses as he goes along.

(Re)search

Facilitation of a group is a (re)search task, to be carried out in several stages.

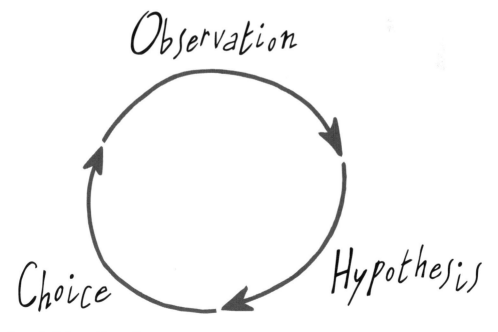

Figure 2 (Re)searching path

- The facilitator adopts an attentive pose and observes what is going on in the group
- On the basis of observation, intuition, and personal theoretical orientation, he draws up a hypothesis
- On the basis of this hypothesis, the facilitator decides on a mode of intervention in the group
- Then the facilitator observes the effects of his intervention, devises new hypotheses, considers possible modes of intervention, and chooses one of them.

> In this cyclical approach, the facilitator adopts an ongoing (re)search stance intended to open up living spaces conducive to the emergence of collective intelligence.

Illustration

How to tell them?

The facilitator may explain the spirit of the '(re)search' to the participants at the outset:

Facilitator (at the beginning of work with a group)

 – *We are going to work all together, in a spirit of 'co-construction', making use of each person's abilities and expertise. We will consider that there is no one right answer and so we will search together. It is for this reason that we are sitting in a semi-circle, without a table, so as to facilitate our interaction and our research. My role as facilitator will be to hold in place a safe frame, to contribute techniques and appropriate spaces for our work so that, all together, we can find answers to your questions.*

Finding out more

The systemic approach draws attention to the fact that there is no single truth, no single right answer, but that numerous options exist, some of which will be more relevant than others at any particular moment. The circularity principle is brought to the fore: a cause may have many effects and an effect may be the outcome of several causes. All connections and interactions between aspects of what is currently happening will be of interest. Operating from within this state of mind, the facilitator will remain constantly animated by the dynamic of the search. Within the group it is not a question of pursuing good or bad options. It is a question, above all, of entering all together into this process of research.

Summary Part 2

In seeking to stimulate collective intelligence, it is vital to nourish the living forces present within a group. The facilitator co-constructs, bringing into play the here and now of whatever is taking place within the group, and in this manner gains access to a process that is in fact already underway.

The reader was introduced to seven key questions for the purpose of activating collective intelligence:

- How am I going to work with the here and now?
- How can I create a safe frame and context?
- How will I stimulate cohesion?
- What can I do to strengthen participants' sense of personal competence?
- How will I take account of what remains unspoken?
- How will I enable the group to see a single situation from different angles?
- How can I remain on a (re)searching path?

PART

3

Five key action techniques for broadening the field of possibilities

Instructions for use of action techniques

- Regard the group and the system as a living process on the move
- Feel before you think
- Show rather than speak
- Represent before solving
- Investigate the 'how' rather than the 'what' or the 'why'
- 'Speak *to*' rather than 'speak *about*'

Jacob Levy Moreno used action methods to invite people to *show* what they were living rather than *tell* it, as a means of enabling them to view the same situation from different angles, through a concrete experience, including body, heart and mind. An action method entails a multifaceted approach to working that includes:

- Movement, experience of the here and now, attention to the body and to feelings

- Direction of attention to inner attitudes

- Reference to a methodological and theoretical basis or background that enables accompaniment of the group process.

The general approach to action methods presented in this book is inspired by the Moreno action method, as well as by additional techniques developed by the authors.

Presentation of the action techniques

Action techniques can be used to tackle any of the questions that arise in working life. For example:

- *How are we to deploy our creativity?*
- *How can the experience of learning be made more alive?*
- *How can we develop this particular project?*
- *What sort of information could help us to move forward?*
- *How can we move beyond the problem we are currently experiencing?*
- *Who is going to do what?*
- *What do we need in order to achieve our goal?*
- *What information is important for enabling us to take a decision?*
- *How could we move towards new working methods?*
- *What kind of organisation is required in order to deal with this change?*

- *How can we achieve better communication?*
- *How can we create a common language?*
- *In what direction are we moving?*
- *How can we resolve this conflict?*

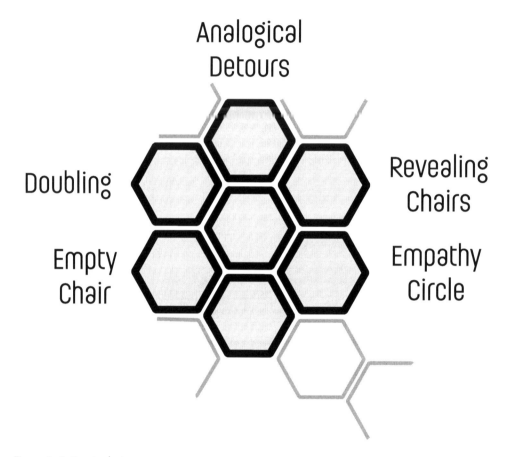

Figure 3 Action techniques

The action techniques developed in this book enable questions such as the preceding to be represented by different means, making use of spatial movement, objects, colours, images, writing, metaphors, etc.

Where do these techniques come from?

Once upon a time in Vienna, in the 1930s, there lived a psychiatrist named Jacob Levy Moreno who developed an unprecedented, surprising, and highly original approach: in the city parks he shouted out to passers-by and enacted scenes from daily life with the help of 'street actors' who came forward to take part. In this way he created, little by little, a kind of spontaneous outdoor theatre in the form of live encounters and performances.

The scenes enacted related to topics chosen together with the participants who came forward: a recent political episode, a family argument, someone who was about to start a new job, etc. Through the use of, in particular, the Role Reversal and Doubling techniques, Jacob Levy Moreno succeeded in stimulating people's spontaneity, prompting them to give expression to things that mattered to them, and to act out their concerns with other people.

He created in this way a number of techniques that encouraged people to play roles and act out life situations, enabling individuals and groups to act out aspects of their inner lives in a manner that included bodily movement and interaction with others.

Jacob Levy Moreno was quite soon joined in this work by his wife, Zerka Toeman Moreno, who made a major theoretical and methodological contribution to the development of this form of action method. The settings devised by Jacob and Zerka Moreno for the pursuit of personal growth provided a vehicle for the action methods. The question that came to be asked was thus not so much *'What happened? Tell me!'*, as *'How did it happen? Show me!'*

Jacob and Zerka Moreno believed that it was necessary, in order to change society, to learn to see a situation through another person's eyes and feelings. Zerka experimented with role reversal in daily life, one example being a mother exchanging roles with her son who refused to drink his soup: the two began laughing together so that mother and child opened up a playful space in which their expression of pleasure enabled the tension to be defused.

The Moreno method was born, initially, of an intuition arising from aspects of daily life observed in the parks of Vienna or in the context of family life. The approach proposed in this book stems directly from the same intuition, seeking to stimulate spontaneity and creativity in the everyday work of group facilitation.

The Moreno action method has spread throughout the world and been adopted in the context of a range of different approaches, in particular the various analytical and systemic movements.

Today the neurosciences have also taken up and confirmed this vital role of the body and of action in the process of personal learning and development. Discoveries concerning how the brain actually works give rise to recommendations to managers, trainers and teachers as to how to get people *actively* involved, prompting them to use bodily movement as a means of helping them move in the direction of their goals.

> This book places Moreno's intuition at the heart of the everyday and stimulates creativity in professional settings and among groups and teams of colleagues. Mobilisation of the body enables people to work on and through certain types of inner process that are otherwise difficult to access.

Finding out more

Jacob Levy Moreno, born in Bucharest in 1889, was brought up in Vienna. During World War I he worked in a refugee camp in Lower Austria where he helped inmates to form groups based on their affinities as a means of surviving their distress. In 1936, having emigrated to the USA a few years earlier, he set up a private clinic with a therapeutic theatre. This was the beginning of Psychodrama.

Moreno's approach has been handled and developed in a variety of ways.

- In the field of therapy, the reference is more usually to Psychodrama – 'psycho' being a reference to mind/spirit/psyche, and the meaning of 'drama', in Greek, being simply 'action'. For Moreno, accordingly, a Psychodrama would be an instance of 'psyche in action'.

- The term Sociodrama is used when it is a question of working specifically on the roles of individuals. Sociodrama deals with situations in which the collective aspects of a problem are brought to the fore, and the question asked in this approach is 'what is my social role in this situation?'

The principal action techniques devised by Moreno are Role Reversal and Doubling. Many others have been created, just a few of which are the Mirror, the Empty Chair, Future Projection, Role Training, Human Sculpture, Soliloquy, or Surplus Reality. Sociometry is a technique that enables visualisation and measurement of the way in which persons in a group, team or organisation become situated in relation to one another, at a specific moment, in a precise situation. The Sociogram is another technique that enables these sociometric findings to be represented on diagrams.

Stimulating collective intelligence

A presentation of the action techniques, including an explanation of their active principles and implementing mechanisms, will link up with all the earlier parts of this book.

The use of action techniques awakens empathy and openness within a group. Their purpose in a collective intelligence setting is thus to steer the group work in a direction and manner that encourages some or all participants to perform work on their own selves.

As outlined in Part 1 of this book, the facilitator's inner stance, the way s/he finds of opening up a space within him/herself, will encourage the group to open up to the task underway through the use of action techniques.

In conjunction with the seven keys described in Part 2 of this book, the action techniques serve as means of stimulating collective intelligence in several different ways:

- They guide people into experience of the here and now (Key 1).

- They require, in order to be effective, the prior setting up of a safety frame (Key 2).

- They foster participant cohesion around a common experience (Key 3).

- They help professionals working in groups to find their own answers to their questions, thereby enhancing their skills and sense of personal competence (Key 4).

- They enable work to take place on aspects that have remained unspoken, thereby helping what has hitherto remained implicit to become explicit (Key 5).

- They enable participants to see a single situation from different angles (Key 6).

- Lastly, they turn the work of facilitation into a 'search' or form of '(re)search' (Key 7).

On entering more deeply into these different aspects, it becomes apparent that, whatever the technique used, whether it is a question of role-playing or of producing a creative representation, there comes a moment at which one or more participants are called upon to make a physical movement or to change place. Simply rising to one's feet triggers a situation quite different from that of people in a group who speak to each other while remaining seated. The nature of the involvement changes.

> The 'empathy stimulus' supplied by seeing a situation from another's standpoint will serve as training for teamworking qualities such as flexibility and agility.

   Movement and, where it takes place, role-playing, bring about a much greater embodiment of thought, capturing the attention of both the person in action and the observers. This setting in motion of a situation makes the work undertaken into a vividly experienced happening for the group in the here and now.

> Which technique will trigger surprise, deeper attention, pleasure and motivation?

   Experience shared or created in common within the group facilitates spoken contributions that spring from a shared form or representation to which each member is able to refer.

   Action techniques are part and parcel of a (re)search process:

- The first stage of this (re)search is observation of what is happening in the here and now.

- As a second step, the facilitator, on the basis of a hypothesis, will choose an appropriate action technique to help the group to see the situation from a different angle.

> New working hypotheses can be considered, new action strategies may emerge, on the personal as well as the relational, group and organisational fronts.

- The facilitator will then observe the effects of what has been experienced, and this will lead him/her forward to other hypotheses, choices for intervention, observation of effects, in an ongoing (re)search process.

Important points to bear in mind when using action methods

To work with spontaneity, proposing contexts for action, is to create a working space in which people will sometimes discard a mask to reveal their true faces. Spontaneity is frequently associated with the expression of some form of vulnerability. For this reason, it is important, as we have seen, to ensure that a safety frame is put in place to enable participants to experience trust. Three particular aspects – ethical considerations to be borne in mind when using action methods – are worth mentioning.

A first important point is to ensure clarity when communicating to the group the boundaries of the work being proposed. The rule of discretion applies equally to the facilitator: of all information pertaining to individual participants and to what they have shared with the group, whether verbally or non-verbally, explicitly or implicitly, only elements that are predominantly general in their nature or that have been validated within the group may be passed on to third parties. Any communication to third parties is thus required to be general in its nature as well as anonymous. The rule of discretion is applicable in order to protect participants from any subsequent leakage of personal information.

At the same time, depending on context, some forms of 'opening' are possible and even desirable. For example, in working with a team of colleagues, to suggest that the hierarchy attend the final part of a session can be a way of fostering a move in the direction of change. The facilitator then becomes a mediator for facilitating circulation of speech and co-construction.

> **Communication**: In relation to the rule of discretion, group members are to be informed in advance of the boundaries between what will and will not be communicated to third parties (hierarchy, team, client, competitor, family, etc.)

A second important point relates to the need to accord full personal consideration to participants and to support their discernment and autonomy. Persons are thus always to be given priority over any technique being used. This means that no interpretation may be allowed to outweigh the discernment of a person or a group. And no technique delivers a single incontrovertible truth. It is the person, or the group, concerned, who are invited to take up a position and who will be allowed the final word.

> **Full consideration**: The feelings, knowledge, representations and speech of the persons concerned are to be regarded as the be-all and end-all of the work.

By way of example: one participant, in an experiment using symbolic objects, realises that she has placed the object that represents her job somewhere to the side on the large sheet that is being used for the experiment. In a voice that betrays her anxiety, she interprets the situation as follows: 'I wonder whether this means that I should leave my job and look for something else'.

The facilitator will be careful to focus on the feelings expressed by the participant and on the meaning she is attributing to having thus seemingly 'set her job aside'. It is always possible to move objects around and to place them differently, and it is the person who has placed these objects in that particular way who remains central to discerning what her choice might mean.

A third important point relates to the criterion of professionalism: every time an action technique is used, effects will ensue in the group. And these effects will be accompanied by, and worked through with, the facilitator. It is important, therefore, that a facilitator practising the action methods should have prior first-hand experience and deep personal

> **Professionalism**: Any technique employed without adequate prior personal experimentation and understanding of its effects risks creating a climate of insecurity for both facilitator and group.

understanding of what is being proposed. Equally important is that the facilitator should have forged links between the techniques being used and her/his own familiar theoretical and methodological apparatus, particularly as it applies to the accompaniment of groups.

Prior arrangement of the workspace

Insofar as participants are willing and space permits, it is preferable to work without a table and with chairs arranged in a circle or semi-circle. If the context allows, a semi-circular arrangement without a table (or with tables pushed together and to one side) fosters interaction and facilitates the organisation of different workspaces, as well as distinguishing space reserved for creative work from that reserved for speech.

If this arrangement is not possible, on practical and logistic grounds or for reasons associated with participants' or organisations' customary ways of working, the facilitator can give preference to whatever arrangement best fosters interaction among participants. Referring back to the chapter on attitudes, it then becomes a question of 'choosing the lesser evil'.

The ARC process: six stages

The ARC process is a tool illustrated in this book and incorporating a set of six separate stages. This tool has been devised in a spirit of close adherence to the approach developed and practised by Moreno.

The name ARC refers to three keywords that characterise work with action techniques:

- A refers to *Action*: Experiencing something in the here and now through the use of action techniques.

- R refers to *Representations*: The ensuing action will enable a single situation to be seen from different angles, thereby amplifying and opening up the field of representations.

- C refers to *Change*. Seeing the same situation from a new angle, and opening up the field of representations, enables a harnessing of new resources for change and innovation.

The ARC process has been devised to enable the simultaneous use of action methods stemming from varying traditions of thought and practice. In this way, the fruits of different disciplines and schools of thought, with their associated practices, are able to prove beneficial in workplace settings as well as in teaching, supervision, coaching, management, and different forms of group facilitation in a range of sectors.

The word 'arc' in French means 'a bow'. Metaphorically speaking, for a facilitator the ARC – or 'bow' – can be a powerful tool and its use requires appropriate training, a clear sense of focus, a methodology and reference points. When holding the bow to shoot an arrow, the body cannot remain rigid; there is a need for a supple form of rootedness. Breathing too is important, for it contributes to presence and concentration.

By analogy with the metaphor of a bow and arrow, the facilitator's work is rooted in supple use of the body and regular practice in adjusting his/her inner posture, using it as a tool, and cultivating non-expectancy, holding to a frame and concentrating on a precise target, all in a spirit of openness.

A facilitator will use the six stages of the ARC process differently, depending on the targets, context and technique being used in any given case. The first stage, that of the safety frame, is nonetheless an essential prerequisite for all work with action methods. In some situations, for example when using the Analogical Detours (see technique 5, Part 3 of the book), Stage 5 (sharing) and Stage 6 (search for paths and action strategies) are not separate. The paths emerge from a process of interweaving creative representations with the group's responses, what is shared, and the links between all this and the question originally asked.

Where the setting is appropriate, particularly in a training context on use of the action techniques, a seventh stage, the feedback stage, is added on in order to discuss the techniques used, the various stages, and the nature of the process that has been experienced and observed. All this is explicitly linked up with the relevant theoretical and methodological components and considerations On the illustration the words in the bubbles are with lower cases. But everywhere else on the other bow illustrations the are mentioned with uppercases. Is it still possible to harmonize ?

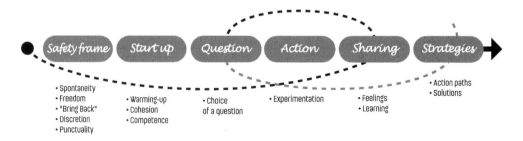

Figure 4 The ARC process

Stage 1: setting up a safety frame

The safety frame referred to in Part 2 (Key 2), inspired by the approach of Jacob Levy Moreno and enriched by that of Carl Gustav Jung, is indispensable for any experience of using action techniques. It is composed of, at the least, the following five working rules:

- The rule of spontaneity (or free thought) is to remind participants that anything and everything may be spoken about, represented, enacted.

- The rule of freedom states that each person is free to accept, or not, any experiment that is proposed. This rule is important because it allows participants to pay attention to their personal comfort zone and to adopt a position in relation to the working proposals suggested by the facilitator.

- The 'bring-back' rule suggests that some information communicated beyond the confines of the group strictly speaking actually *belongs* to the group and is of sufficient worth to merit its subsequent voicing and communication in the group as a whole.

- The rule of discretion can be represented, for example, by the confidentiality circle referred to in Reference sheet 25.

- The punctuality rule is important in the practice of action techniques because, for a facilitator, there may be a tendency to become carried away by what is happening in the here and now. A strict and yet at the same time supple observance of a schedule will provide a container for the work. Respect for a timetable is one component of a holding experience, insofar as it wordlessly communicates the message that every task has a beginning and an end.

Stage 2: start-up

- The facilitator chooses how s/he is going to organise the warming-up component of the session, in what ways to prepare persons to open up to one another, to move around in the space available and to set in motion their physical and mental energy (Reference sheet 31).

- The facilitator seeks to make clear how the persons are connected to each other. For this purpose s/he may, for example, ask participants to gather in sub-groups for an exchange to discover connections. Attention to this notion of connection will increase cohesion within the group (Reference sheet 6).

- The facilitator ensures that in starting up the work, s/he places the accent on the numerous and diverse forms of competence contained within the group, for example by inviting participants to speak about their own talents, experience, what they actually do or know how to do (Reference sheet 7).

Stage 3: question stage

The facilitator gathers together the contexts, situations, difficulties and questions presented by the group. Questions may be of relevance to one person in the group, to several persons, or to the group as a whole. When the question comes from one or several persons within the group, the facilitator observes and comments upon whether and how it may be of relevance to the group as a whole. Sociometry is a technique stemming from Moreno's action method which offers the group the possibility of itself deciding on an order of priority or a choice as to the questions that the group will tackle.

> When a question is tackled using the action techniques, the group will enter a state of 'resonance'.

Stage 4: action stage

Faced with a question, it is possible to seek an answer or a solution directly. Another option is to allow oneself a period of experimentation in the form of a detour that allows the situation in question to be viewed from different angles. This experimental detour solicits the creative imagination, thereby enabling the creation of information. The search for action paths and strategies is then nourished by this detour. The use of action techniques is intended to propose experimentation along these lines, in relation to the question that has been chosen. Depending on which technique is used, the stimulation of the senses differs. And while certain techniques may be more relevant than others at any given moment, it would be restrictive to lay down excessively specific rules concerning the choice of one technique rather than another. This choice is made in a specific context, making use of whatever is happening here and now in the group.

Whereas some techniques make use of objects and symbolic dimensions, others are based on role-playing. Some techniques are more appropriate for exploring the dynamic of an individual person and others are more suited to working with the context. Some techniques call for a setting in motion of the group as a whole, while others call for just one or two group members to move or change places. Some techniques entail work in sub-groups. Depending on the facilitator's perception of the group with which s/he is working, s/he can thus choose the technique likely to prove most acceptable to the group and most useful at this precise moment in the process.

> The facilitator places him/herself in a (re)search dynamic, observing what is happening in the group, drawing up a hypothesis, choosing a technique, observing its effects, and so forth.

Stage 5: sharing stage

During this sharing stage, participants are invited to place in common what they have experienced, what has been important for them, and what they have learned of value to themselves during the action period. In some cases, in order to be able to derive benefit from the work with the action techniques, the facilitator does well to preserve and prolong this space of sharing, ensuring that it is not too quickly replaced by Stage 6 of searching for action paths and strategies.

Stage 6: action paths and strategies

Participants exchange and begin to search for action paths and strategies in relation to the original question. It is possible to organise this search in different ways. When one person is more particularly concerned by the question being tackled, one option is to ask her to 'stand back' while the other group members search on her behalf, and then to give her the floor so that she can state her position.

It is important to note that, in some situations, for example when using the Analogical Detours (see technique 5, part 3 of the book), Stage 5 (sharing) and Stage 6 (search for paths and action strategies) are not separate. The paths emerge from a process of interweaving creative representations with the group's responses, what is shared, and the links between all this and the question originally asked.

Role of the 'action facilitator'

When groups and work teams are open to and prepared for the use of action techniques, for example in the framework of a staff meeting in the workplace, one person will play the role of 'action facilitator'.

The role of facilitator can be played by an external professional facilitator who accompanies the group and has been, so to speak, 'mandated' to facilitate the group process. Whether or not the group is accompanied by such an external facilitator, the hat of 'action facilitator' can be attributed to a member of the group.

It is important that the 'action facilitator' should be sufficiently familiar with the use of the technique that he is launching and know how to handle the whole process of using action techniques (cf. ARC process). Other important points to bear in mind when using action methods mentioned earlier should also be taken into account, such as the need to establish clear communication concerning the work boundaries, to give full consideration to individuals, and to adopt an appropriately professional stance in handling the situation.

The role of the 'action facilitator' is to:

- Check that the group agrees to work with this particular action technique.
- Introduce the action technique, explaining how it works.
- Ensure that experimentation with the technique takes place within some appropriate broader process. This book gives precedence to the ARC process, consisting of a number of stages, and which may be used differently depending on context.
- Launch the action technique.

Each member of a group may suggest the use of action techniques. It is undoubtedly the case that to bring experimentation into a professional setting is to bring in an element of informality, an element of 'as if', of movement, and this may call for 'daring' on the part of the person proposing the technique while at the same time requesting permission from the rest of the group.

In the following pages, experiences taken 'from the field', illustrated and coloured by different group facilitation contexts, will enable better integration of the different stages of the work with the action techniques. As the experiences in the field illustrated represent moments separated out from a process, not every stage of the work will be included in every example.

Depending on the different contexts and techniques, some stages receive more attention than others, with the exception of Stage 1 which advocates the safety frame that is an indispensable basis for any work with action techniques.

Technique 1: Doubling

How can a person or a group be helped to clarify a question, seek ways to a solution, a thought, a non-verbal expression, an aim or target?

> The Doubling technique, as created by Jacob Levy Moreno, is used when one person seeks, by means of empathy, to enact the experience or thinking of another person while standing close to him or her.

Use of Doubling

The work of doubling illustrated in Figure 5 can take place in either of two forms, either 'spontaneously' or 'sequentially'.

Figure 5 Doubling technique

Spontaneous version

The facilitator proposes at some point during the session to double one or more persons from the group. At this point in the here and now the facilitator hypothesises that doubling might be a way of helping the group to move in the direction of its aim or target.

Sequential version

A portion of the working time is devoted to doubling as an organised exercise in itself. Several members of the group will be given the opportunity to double other members.

Whether doubling is practised in the sequential or the spontaneous version, it is an element in a process as described in the ARC. It will be relevant during some stages more than others (except during Stage 1, the safety frame, which is an essential prerequisite for all action methods).

When using the Doubling technique, the facilitator begins by requesting the consent of the person she wishes to double, after which she gets up, moves close to this person and, always with his consent, says something, in a standing position, in the other's place. The 'double' helps another person to express what he or she feels and yet does not dare to say or cannot manage to put into words. It could be something that is mixed up, taboo, perhaps only semi-conscious, possibly even unconscious.

Once the 'double' has put something into words, the person being 'doubled' is invited to say whether what the 'double' has said corresponds to his own feelings or thoughts. More often than not, the person who has been 'doubled' confirms, either by agreeing with the general drift or by stating that something different is the case, that the 'double' has provided some relevant 'food for thought'.

In this way, the person who has been doubled can correct, complete, or acquiesce, thereby clarifying and sharpening the question that he has put to the group. The fact that there has been a movement, that one person has stood up to move close to another and speak in his place, will serve to channel the attention of both the group and the person being doubled.

When a person 'doubles' another, she takes up a role because she places herself to some extent in the place of this other person. And one effect of taking up a role is to lead her to become in some way detached from herself as a means of becoming closer to the person she is doubling in the place where he is to be found.

In order to position himself, the person who has been doubled devises and finds directions.

Pragmatically speaking, the experience of doubling may also be used to assist in the formulation of aims, questions or action paths.

Points for attention

- Before doubling, it is essential to request consent from the person in question and, after the doubling, he will be asked to take up a position on what has been said in his place.

- If the person who wishes to double is not the facilitator, she should request the facilitator's consent for her proposal for a doubling.

- Doubling may be conducted by only one person at a time.

- The person doubling may, if she wishes, place her hand on the shoulder of the one who is being doubled. However, before initiating physical contact, permission must be asked of the person one is doubling. An alternative is to place one's hand a few centimetres away from the doubled person's shoulder, without touching it. Doubling may also take place without any movement of the hand in the direction of the person being doubled.

- It is possible to double a group. In this case the facilitator walks around the group and says something aloud 'in place of the group'. The group can then react, take up a position, clarify specific points, express its responses.

Illustration

Choosing: leading a project, making choices

Facilitator's hypothesis: the Doubling technique could enable Peter to put his ambivalence into words and perhaps come to adopt a different stance.

The facilitator, in the framework of a management training session, hears what Peter has to say about hesitations in the face of various possible options in the conduct of a project. Peter states that he is feeling rather lost and can no longer see clearly what direction he should take. The facilitator suggests that a doubling exercise might help Peter to find a way of putting his ambivalence more clearly into words.

Facilitator (to Peter):

– *Peter, would you agree to be 'doubled'?*

Peter:

– *To be what?!?* (laughing)

Facilitator (to Peter)

– *It would mean that, with your consent, several people, one at a time, would come close to you and would speak in your place. Each time you will have a feeling of whatever it may be that their words evoke within you. I would propose that, after each 'doubling', you begin by simply saying 'I take that*

> *on board' or 'I don't take it on board'. That doesn't prevent you, if you wish, from making some additional comment to correct or fill out what has been said.*

Peter:

> – *OK let's give it a try.*

Facilitator (to group):

> – *So now it's up to you. When you want to try out a doubling, you begin by asking Peter whether he agrees to let you double him. If he says yes, you stand up and move close to him. You may, if you wish, ask Peter whether he agrees to let you place your hand on his shoulder. That can be helpful, but it is not essential. Then you speak aloud, saying something in Peter's place. Peter, you remain seated, and allow yourself to feel whatever is happening inside you.*

Participant A:

> – *Peter, is it OK if I double you?*

Peter:

> – *Go ahead.*

Participant A (standing, next to Peter, with one hand on Peter's shoulder):

> – *I, Peter, would choose to, first, contact my client to discuss the various possible options and then ask him which he prefers.*

Peter:

> – *Taken.*

Participant B:

> – *Can I double you too?*

Peter:

> – *Well yes!*

Participant B (standing close to Peter):

> – *I, Peter, will ask the opinion of at least two close colleagues before taking any decision.*

Peter:

> – *Point taken, except that I actually think we should hold a meeting of the whole team.*

Five other participants have a try at doubling and, in each case, Peter takes up a position.

Facilitator (to Peter):

– *After this experience of doubling, Peter, where are you now? What is your position at this point? What is your message to the group?*

Peter:

– *It is surprising how the contact of a hand on my shoulder helped me to gather my thoughts and put me in touch with my feelings even though I was not the one putting them into words. So I found I gained support from the experience, and hearing so many opinions helped me to see things more clearly, even though I can't now remember everything that was said. I'm now more convinced than ever that I need to speak openly in a meeting about this situation and the choice to be made.*

Finding out more

The earliest experiences of the child with the persons closest to him are highly relevant to the experience of doubling. The people around him spontaneously name or wordlessly represent the baby's inner world, his needs, feelings and actions. This interaction gives shape and meaning to what the child is experiencing and would be unable to express on his own. This is how a relation of empathy grows up between the child and the adult, providing a setting for the child's growth.

Technique 2: the Empty Chair

How to open up a space in which one can allow oneself to be surprised by a piece of new information

> The Empty Chair is a technique used in different 'schools' of counselling or facilitation practice. Its purpose is to open up a virtual space for a 'key partner' by positioning an empty chair so as to represent that person or entity. Participants stand up and go to stand behind the empty chair where they 'lend their voice' to the 'partner' represented by this empty chair. This technique can be usefully employed, for example, in an office meeting.

Figure 6 Empty Chair technique

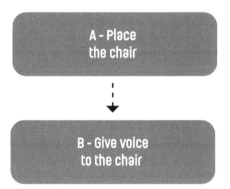

Figure 7 How to use Empty Chair

Using the Empty Chair

As in every facilitation process, the safety frame, or Stage 1, is an initial prerequisite. The Empty Chair technique, as illustrated in Figures 6 and 7, can be used, for example, during an office meeting. The mere presence of this empty chair, because of the entity or person that it is intended to represent, will serve to jolt ingrained thinking patterns and generate new information.

Facilitator:

- *I propose that a volunteer should stand up and come to stand behind the empty chair that I am placing here, which represents our company. And then the volunteer, speaking on behalf of the firm, will say something.*

Participants say something on behalf of whatever/whomever is represented by the chairs. In this way, the chairs carry the voice of the persons or entities that they have been designated to represent.

> An empty chair is brought in to represent, for example, a person, a group, an organisation, who/which is 'given voice'. This experiment encourages spontaneity and fosters creativity.

People often spontaneously, while speaking, place their hands on the back of the chair. This physical contact with the chair can be a way of helping them enter into the role of whatever or whomever the chair has been placed there to represent.

Each time someone gets up to give voice to the chair, all the group members experience a form of movement within themselves. Because, here too, the activation process *makes* something happen.

And when there are, for example, tensions within a team, and the facilitator, with the group's consent, places an empty chair to represent the company of which the team is a part, a space for 'play' is opened up. Indirectly, the chair that represents the company becomes a 'third party', enabling speech to circulate differently and more freely than in a tense and direct relationship among the individuals actually present.

As an exercise or throughout the meeting

The introduction of a chair can take place in two ways, as either a 'spontaneous version' or a 'sequential version'.

Spontaneous version

Without any specific question necessarily having been raised at the outset, a member of the group, or the group itself, decides to include an empty chair in the meeting venue as a means of fostering a degree of detachment. It may be decided that this chair represents a person, a group, an organisation, an entity or a concept that is significant in the context of this particular meeting.

Facilitator:

– *And so, we have added this chair which represents our company. At any point during our meeting, you should, if you so wish, feel free to stand up and come forward to give voice to this chair.*

Sequential version

One section of the meeting time is formally set aside for giving voice to the empty chair.

Of all the action techniques entailing role-taking proposed in this book, the Empty Chair is the easiest to use in the framework of a workplace meeting.

Facilitator:

– *We are going to devote a quarter of an hour to giving voice to the chair that represents our company. Anyone who so wishes may get up, come to stand behind the chair, and say something 'on behalf of the company'. We could also, if you agree, do this by each coming forward in turn. Afterwards, we will talk about what happened.*

One person takes on the role of 'action facilitator'

Use of an action technique in a workplace meeting requires that the team be prepared for involvement along these lines. In work settings where the staff are already adequately prepared, the empty chair is sometimes used as and when appropriate, without external facilitators, by groups of colleagues who opt to use it as a way

In a workplace meeting where use is to be made of the empty chair, one person plays the role of 'action facilitator'.

of making their meetings livelier. In this specific situation, it is important that one person should take on the role of 'action facilitator'. This role may, what is more, be introduced in the same way as that of 'timekeeper' or 'chairperson' and can be taken from one meeting to another by a different person.

The role of 'action facilitator' is, first of all, to check that the group consents to use this technique. Having ensured that this is the case, he introduces the chair, explaining its purpose and how it will be used.

In a 'sequential version', the person playing the role of 'action facilitator' remains standing, and this is already a non-verbal invitation to others to stand up to speak on behalf of whatever or whomever the chair is placed there to represent.

In a 'spontaneous version', during the meeting the 'action facilitator' will, at regular intervals, remind the team of the possibility of speaking on behalf of whatever the chair represents. At the end of the meeting, he will remove the chair and ask group members to state whether and in what ways they found the experimentation with the chair to be useful.

In both cases, whether in the 'sequential version' or the 'spontaneous version', the 'action facilitator' may contribute some opening comments and questions suggesting possible hypotheses so as to start participants' thinking. To do this, he will stand up, move close to the person who has taken up the role behind the chair and speak in the first person singular (i.e. in terms of 'I'). In this way, he accompanies the person who has taken up the role to speak in place of what the chair represents. For example:

Facilitator (standing next to the person who has just been speaking on behalf of the chair):

- *'I, the company, observe that . . .'.* (stimulus in the form of opening comment)
- Or *'What is my ambition as a company?'* (stimulus in the form of a question)

Participant (standing behind the chair)

- *'I observe that . . . our staff members have run out of steam'.*
- Or *'my ambition is to innovate'.*

If, for any reason, participants do not get up to come to speak behind the empty chair, the 'action facilitator' may decide, with the consent of the group, to stand there to repeat, behind the chair, proposals that have been made by participants from their seats. The 'action facilitator' then speaks on behalf of whatever the chair represents, in this case the company, taking up some of the suggestions made earlier by participants.

Points for attention

- Request the group's consent before using this technique.
- When several persons are going to play a role and circulation of speech is to be facilitated using the empty chair, it is suggested that the facilitator remain standing behind the chair rather than sitting down. The fact that role-players do not actually sit down on the chair enables a succession of people to come forward to speak in quick succession. Each one 'touches' the role and then moves away quickly, enabling another person to take up the same role immediately afterwards and say something different.

- The experiment may be organised differently if the aim is not that several persons should play the same role. When it is intended that one participant remain longer in a role, to dwell on and explore it, then the facilitator may suggest that the person taking the role might sit down on the chair.

- The act of getting up and going to stand behind the empty chair, of sensing what is happening in silence and with one's hands placed on the chair back, is already in itself an experience that constitutes a source of information. An alternative can be to not ask the chair to speak but merely to feel what is happening in that place where the chair is standing. The facilitator can make a point of paying attention to this 'sensing' dimension when a person comes to stand or sit in the place where s/he is taking a role.

Illustrations

Vision: developing a vision

The facilitator is at the start of a day-long session with a European association that brings its members together three times a year in order to link up with projects being conducted in the different countries, to develop their thinking in common, and to decide on both a set of general guidelines and a vision to be built up or consolidated.

After the first stage of establishing the safety frame, the facilitator decides to add an empty chair to represent the association.

The question at the heart of the team's concerns is:

— *How can we strengthen the spirit of cooperation in relation to specific projects?*

Facilitator:

— *If you all agree, we will use the option of coming forward to speak behind the empty chair that represents our association. When you so wish, I suggest that you stand up, come to stand behind the empty chair, possibly placing your hands on its back, and that you say out loud whatever words come to you as you imagine yourself to be speaking on behalf of our association.*

Facilitator's hypothesis: adding an empty chair to represent the association and thereby offering the opportunity for participants to speak on its behalf could serve to foster cohesion within the group.

> – *This may be something about the current challenges, about what our association might be feeling or thinking, any messages that it would like us to heed . . . and I would propose that each contribution along these lines should begin with the words 'This is what I, the association, am experiencing, what I think about the situation, this is the message I want to give you'.*

The facilitator stands up and thus provides physical accompaniment to participants while supplying prompts in the form of questions:

Facilitator (standing next to the participant who has stood up and come to stand behind the empty chair):

> – *For how long have I been in existence as an association?*

Participant (behind the chair):

> – *For 40 years.*

Facilitator:

> – *How am I, the association, feeling in this meeting?*

Participant (behind the chair):

> – *I feel that I am beset by numerous challenges.*

Facilitator:

> – *What do I need if I am to continue to exist?*

Participant (behind the chair):

> – *Someone to set my finances in better order, some clarification of exactly what I am supposed to be doing, some steps that will serve to enhance my visibility.*

Facilitator:

> – *What is my mission?*

After each question, the person who has taken the role of the association can take note of his own feelings, allow something to rise to the surface and be spoken in response to the facilitator's promptings. It is a situation in which something comes alive in the here and now and which draws the attention of not only the person playing the role but all those observing.

In this particular example, after Stage 5 (sharing) and Stage 6 (search for action paths and strategies), a focus on the technique used (here the Empty Chair) enabled several participants to express what they had experienced:

- *The fact that there was an empty chair to represent the association enabled me to concentrate on the subject of our meeting.*

- *It gave me pleasure to 'play' and to spend time together with my colleagues in this way.*

- *It helped me to gain some distance in relation to some rather sensitive subjects.*

- *It meant that we could hear other colleagues' points of view expressed somehow in a new way.*

- *I really love being able to think 'out of the box'; it makes us so much more creative!*

- *It is an interesting technique that I may perhaps be able to use again with my staff team; this chair could represent, for example, our clientele taken as a whole.*

Change: a change of director

A director, after twenty years in his post, is standing down to take his retirement. A new director has been recruited. With the facilitator, three sessions have been organised together with the staff for the purpose of ensuring a smooth transition.

The focus for the work is thus the following question:

- *How can we facilitate the handover by the former director to his successor?*

The facilitator's hypothesis is that if the team members can experience putting themselves in the new director's place and he can experience putting himself in the place of the team, they will together be able to create the beginnings of a common history.

The work was to take place in three sessions. The choice proposed by the facilitator was as follows: the first two working sessions would take place with the team and the new director, in the absence of the former director. The third session would take place in the presence of the team, the new director *and* the former director.

> Facilitator's hypothesis: working with an empty chair in a safe setting could allow each party to the process (staff team, new director) the opportunity to stand in the other's shoes and thus to develop a form of mutual empathy.

- Session 1: staff + new director. The former director was not present. The staff were invited to create a wall chart showing the important moments in the history of their organisation. Some time was devoted to gazing at this chart in silence to take every-thing in and exchange views on what individuals had been struck by, aspects to which each person had been particularly sensitive.

This experiment was intended to prompt the staff, in presence of the new director, to look back over the history and origins of the organisation, including elements both 'symbolic' and 'real'. Information would in this way circulate concerning different events that had been of significance through the course of time.

- Session 2: staff + new director. The former director was not present at this session either. An empty chair was placed in the meeting area to represent the former director. In the presence of the new director, the facilitator suggested that any staff members who so wished should come to speak from behind the chair representing the former director. This stage of the proceedings enabled the new director to receive, indirectly, information that might be useful to him, about the institution's history. The instruction given was as follows:

Facilitator:

- *Anyone who so wishes may get up and come to stand behind the empty chair that represents the former director, and there say something on behalf of the former director.*

The facilitator was standing close to the empty chair representing the former director, accompanying in this way each of the staff members who came up to speak 'on behalf of' the former director.

Staff members stood up and came to speak 'as if' they were the former director, stand-ing behind the empty chair. The facilitator encouraged and accompanied the role-taking by issuing prompts:

Facilitator (standing next to the person who had come to speak from behind the empty chair):

- *What have been my achievements as former director?*

Participant (giving voice to the empty chair):

- *I created this institution. Without me, it would not exist. Initially there were four of us managing the project and now there are fifty of us. I'm rather proud of this.*

Facilitator (standing next to another participant who had come to speak from behind the empty chair representing the former director):

- *During my time as director, what factors inspired my action?*

Participant (giving voice to the empty chair representing the former director):

– *I always believed that, in the face of setbacks, it was essential to bounce back. We experienced two major financial crises, we were forced to make some of our staff redundant, and there were times when I asked myself what was the point of carrying on the fight and putting so much energy into my work as director . . . . At the same time, deep down, I do believe in our project. I find it meaningful and I feel that we have always remained creative. So that belief is what has enabled me to keep going!*

Other possible prompts from the facilitator to assist the role-taking might have been:

– *What values were most important to me in my position as director?*

– *In what way did I feel responsible for the projects?*

– *What is the success of which I am most proud?*

After this experiment, some time was devoted to speaking about what had taken place. This is the sharing stage during which the facilitator asks participants to share their feelings, say what they themselves have learned, and offer their observations in relation to the role-playing.

• Session 3: staff team + new director + former director. An empty chair was placed in the centre of the work area. This time it represented the new director. The team members, in the presence of the new director, were encouraged to come to stand behind the empty chair and to say something from the imagined standpoint of the new director.

In being offered the opportunity to take the role of the new director, or to observe other participants who took up this role, the team members expressed their expectations and in some cases their fears. Here too, the facilitator was standing next to the empty chair to accompany the role-playing and supply prompts along the following lines:

Facilitator (standing beside a participant who had come up to speak beside the empty chair representing the new director):

– *As new director, what are my needs?*

Participant (lending her voice to the empty chair that represents the new director):

– *What I need . . . is to be allowed some time in which to find my place . . . I need . . . to be given all relevant information.*

Facilitator (standing beside another participant who came to speak behind the empty chair representing the new director):

– *What questions do I have as new director?*

Participant (speaking from behind the empty chair representing the new director):

– *I'm wondering what the team's habits are in relation to distribution of tasks, I'm wondering whether the subsidies will be enough for us to take on new staff, I'm wondering how often staff meetings are held.*

Here too, other prompts could have been supplied by the facilitator to assist the role-taking. For example:

– *What are my intentions concerning the transition phase between old and new director?*

– *What are my expectations as I set out in my new post as director?*

– *What are my wishes in relation to the institutional project?*

Each time the person coming forward to take the role of the new director replied. The prompts served to restore the flow of speech when it stalled. Role-taking could also take place spontaneously without prompts from the facilitator. However, the facilitator remained always standing to accompany the process, intervene, and ask a question if and when necessary.

In the course of this experiment, some of the interventions were along the lines of a comparison between the new director and the former director. From what he heard, the new director was able to take up a position and say whether what he was hearing corresponded or not to his own perception of his role. After this experience, time was set aside for participants to share their responses to what had taken place.

After having played the role of the new director in his presence, the staff members could no longer have the same relationship which him, because they had 'experienced' something of the situation in which the new director found himself. They were experiencing something in common and communication was enhanced by the expression of subjective manners of considering the situation.

> Coming forward to speak from behind the empty chair enables the creation of information. It is a way of enabling things to be expressed that were present and implicit but had not yet been made manifestly explicit.

Three sessions were devoted to work on participants' diverse representations, to accompany change, and thereby set in motion a common narrative: is this time wasted when one considers the importance, for the successful conduct of projects, of relations between a staff team and its leadership?

Finding out more

Frédéric Laloux in his well-known book *Reinventing organisations*, illustrates one way of using the Empty Chair technique in office meetings. Here it is a question of suggesting that anyone who so wishes should come up to speak behind the empty chair at any point in the meeting as a way of giving voice to the company by becoming its spokesperson. The facilitator can trigger the role-taking using prompts along, for example, the following lines:

– *In what direction do I, the company, wish to move and at what speed?*

– *Do I, the company, consider that we are being excessively bold? Or not daring enough?*

– *Are there other things that I, the company, would like to bring up for discussion?*

– *Do I, the company, believe that the decisions that have been taken are beneficial? What is my position now that the meeting is coming to a close?*

– *What kind of conclusions would I, as the company, draw from this meeting? What would I say has been achieved here today?*

Technique 3: the Empathy Circle

How to enable a group to experience empathy in a manner sufficiently strong to help it move forward

The Empathy Circle is a technique created by Chantal Nève-Hanquet. When working with the Empathy Circle, participants sit in a circle without a table. An empty chair is placed close to the facilitator. One person stands up and comes to sit on this chair. The facilitator, and then other members of the group, put questions to this participant, asking them in the first person singular ('I'), so as to help him or her to enter a role.

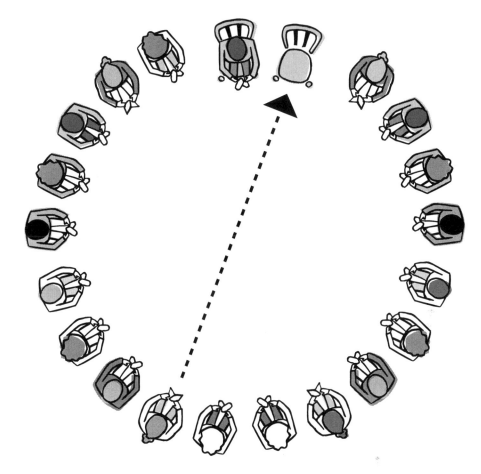

Figure 8 Empathy Circle technique

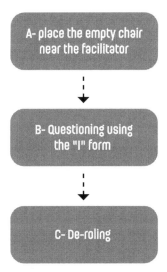

Figure 9 How to use the Empathy Circle

Using the Empathy Circle

The Empathy Circle technique stimulates the sense of the other, that is the capacity to take into account the relational needs of another person and his or her emotional and behavioural features. This technique gives a person the opportunity to play the role of a third person who is of significance for him or herself.

The Empathy Circle serves to bring about inner movement within persons and within the group, while requiring a very small amount of physical changing of places. As shown in Figures 8 and 9, participants can remain in their own seats. Only the person taking on a role changes place and comes to sit on a spare chair that has been placed next to the facilitator. Questions are asked in the first person singular, i.e. using the 'I' form, as illustrated in the following examples. The Empathy Circle will place all group participants at an equal level of participation, since each one asks questions or at least has the opportunity to do so.

In the Empathy Circle experiment, participants start out from what they know about the person whose role they will play and then see what happens. Senior staff, for example, play the role of a more junior colleague, jobseekers take the role of the potential employer, doctors play the role of patients, teachers of their pupils, producers of their customers, psychologists of their clients, and so forth.

This technique is always used to play the role of someone who is not physically present. Frequently, this will be a person with whom the roleplayer has a difficult or complex relationship. By way of example, if I am a social worker and want to put in place a project for someone for whose care I am responsible, the experience of playing the role of this other person will generate some useful information. This methodology allows me to come closer to the person – in this case a person for whose care I am responsible – in that person's own setting, as a means of coming to understand him or her better with a view to establishing a different relationship.

In playing the role of a person with whom one has a difficult relationship, or a relationship that raises significant questions, one supplies – to oneself and the group – information that is useful for the next stage of the work. On subsequently meeting again the person whose role one has played, one will approach that person differently in the wake of the role-playing experience.

> It often happens that in the wake of an Empathy Circle, professionals observe a change. The relationship with the person whose role they have played is no longer quite as it was before.

In a process that has begun with a safety frame (Stage 1), and when the facilitator has also taken care of the start-up (Stage 2), he will help the group to identify a situation in which the relationship between two people seems to be in some way problematic (Stage 3). This may be a situation in which the relationship is strained or one on which a great deal depends. The facilitator will then help the group to formulate the initial question. The Empathy Circle corresponds to Stage 4, that of action or experimentation.

The Empathy Circle technique takes place in three phases:

Phase A: propose the role-playing and then place the empty chair near the facilitator

Facilitator (to John, the participant most closely affected by the initial question):

- *John, do you agree to make Alice present, with my help and that of the group as a whole?*

John, if he has agreed, will come to sit on the empty chair. We thus have here a physical movement in space.

Facilitator (to John who has agreed to play the role of Alice):

- *I would suggest that you come to sit on the chair beside me. I will ask you a few questions which I would like you to answer using the 'I' – first person singular – form as if you were Alice whose role you are playing.*

Phase B: role-playing

Facilitator (to group)

- *We are going to put some questions to John who has agreed to play the role of Alice. We will ask him our questions using the 'I' form. I will ask the first questions and then I would ask any members of the group who so wish to ask whatever questions come into their minds.*

Facilitator:

- *What is MY name?*

John (in the role of Alice):

- *My name is Alice.*

Facilitator:

- *How old am I?*

John (in the role of Alice):

- *I am a 40-year-old woman.*

Facilitator:

- *What am I wearing today?*

John (in the role of Alice):

- *I am wearing my favourite black skirt with a green sweater.*

Facilitator:

- *For how long have I been working here?*

It is important to begin with questions that are simple, matter-of-fact, that enable the person playing the role to enter into that role. Little by little, the questions may become broader and thereby enable the person playing the role and the participants to gain access to other more complex information, for example:

- *What would the boss say about what he sees as my qualities?*
- *How do I remember my first day of work here?*
- *What is my most memorable experience as a member of this work team?*
- *What do I feel inclined to say about difficulties I experience?*

The questions that emerge from the group are always of great interest because they open up the exploration. Indeed, they are based on the various hypotheses that people construct, gradually, and on their own experience. Each participant must necessarily set aside his or her own representations to place himself in the service of the person who is playing the role.

Phase C: coming out of the role (de-roling)

In the Empathy Circle technique, the de-roling takes place in three stages. These three stages each have their own subtle and specific nuance in order to accompany the person who has taken on a role, to guide him/her in exiting this role, one stage at a time. De-roling is a stage that enables the creation of important information in the search for action paths and strategies.

- Step 1 of de-roling: feelings experienced in the role

When the 'I questioning' is finished, the facilitator changes place with the person who has played a role. This is a first step in detachment, the aim of which is to give the person who has played a role the opportunity to state how s/he felt in this role, while still remaining connected to the role.

Facilitator (to John playing the role of Alice):

> *We are going to change places. You come to sit on my chair and I sit on yours. Now that we have changed places, tell me, John, how did you feel in the place of Alice whose role you have been playing? What went on inside you as you were playing this role?*

- Step 2 of de-roling: coming out of the role

Facilitator (to John playing the role of Alice):

> *John, now I am going to ask you to stand up, to come out of the role, to leave the empty chair here and to go back to your original place in the circle. As you return there, state your name very clearly and loudly!*

The facilitator accompanies and encourages the person in de-roling, for example in asking him/her to say his/her name out loud, to stamp his feet, shake his arms and his hands or rub hard on his clothes. This stage, described in Reference sheet 9, is important. There are cases in which participants, imbued with the intensity of what they have experienced during the role-playing, need more time and transition rituals in order to come out of the role they have been playing.

- Step 3 of de-roling: what was felt in playing the role

Facilitator (to John who played the role of Alice):

- *Now that you have returned to your place, John, how do you feel? And what was it like for you playing Alice's role?*

These three steps of the de-roling process are worth taking seriously as a means of deriving benefit from the experience of the person who has played a role and of making it explicit.

The facilitator then addresses the group for the period of sharing, which is Stage 5 of the ARC process.

Facilitator (to the group):

- *What was important for you in this experience?*

After the time set aside for sharing, the facilitator returns to the initial question as formulated during Stage 3 of the ARC process so as to then lead the group into Stage 6, the search for action paths and strategies. The work ends with the setting aside of the empty chair by the person who has played the role. The act of putting away the chair is part of the de-roling. The chair is restored to its status of 'chair'.

> The rhythm of the questions creates a movement, a density, a space that is inhabited because each of the persons in it has turned their thoughts and feelings inwards.

Points for attention

- First request the group's consent before using this technique.
- When using the Empathy Circle technique, it is important, so as to enable the work to take place with the requisite degree of detachment, that the person whose role is being played should not be physically in the room.
- It can happen that, without realizing it, the person who has taken on a role slips out of the role and begins to speak on his or her own behalf. If the facilitator suspects that

this may have happened, she can check up on the situation by asking *'would he (or she) say what you are now saying?'*

- The facilitator should take care to ensure that the other members of the group stick to the form of questioning that uses the first person singular and do not become diverted into other forms of communication, such as:

    - Starting up a dialogue with the person who has taken on a role but addressing her/him in the second person singular as 'you'.

    - Starting to make comments or to analyse what is going on. This part of the experiment is devoted exclusively to helping the person who has taken on a role to enter into this role.

- It is sometimes important to reaffirm that the person one is representing is not the real person and that the aim is to bring him or her into existence through the representations of the person who is playing the role.

- The arrangement in a circle (without a table) contributes to creating a feeling of safety, while helping participants to feel connected to one another. If it is not possible to use this arrangement in a circle, the participants can also be allowed to remain seated around a table. The only thing that must not be left out is the addition of an empty chair so that the person who is playing a role is obliged to change place and not remain on his or her own chair. This 'detail' is important both to facilitate the taking up of a role (en-roling) and the letting go of it (de-roling).

Illustration

Manager: moving over to a computerised system

The facilitator is supervising a group of heads of department. In this group, Barbara, who is in charge of a local government service department, raises the following problematic case:

Barbara:

- *Lise, a civil servant working under my supervision, is just a year away from retirement and refuses to alter her way of working. She is extremely reluctant to learn to use the new computerised systems. I feel quite powerless in the face of such a mass of inert refusal.*

Facilitator (to Barbara):

- *What is your question in relation to this situation?*

Barbara:

–   *What can be done to motivate colleagues who exhibit a 'what's the point?' stance, who have 'always worked like this' and have no desire to move in the direction of change?*

As this is a problem that entails relationship with another person, the facilitator suggested that the Empathy Circle might be a way of helping Barbara and the group to gain a closer understanding of what was happening to Lise while at the same time enabling them to gain some distance.

> Facilitator's hypothesis: the Empathy Circle will enable the situation to be viewed from the standpoint of Lise, enabling participants to gain some distance and thereby open up the field of possibilities.

Facilitator (to Barbara):

–   *Do you agree to play the role of Lise?*

Barbara:

–   *Yes*

Facilitator:

–   *(To the group) We are going to put some questions to Barbara who will play the role of Lise. And after each question asked, Barbara will answer.*

–   *(To Barbara) Barbara, if there's a question you don't know how to answer, you can just say nothing, or imagine what Lise might reply.*

–   *(To all) This is an experiment in which each participant moves inside him or herself and allows him or herself to feel what questions might be asked. It is rather as if we were bringing Lise into existence through the representations of Barbara.*

–   *(To the group) I will ask the first questions. Then you, the group, will yourselves ask questions using the first person singular, the 'I' form. And Barbara will reply.*

The facilitator added a chair next to his own and asked participants to sit in a circle, each one remaining seated on his or her chair. Barbara came to sit on the chair next to the facilitator. The chair on which she had been sitting earlier now remained empty in the circle. The facilitator began by asking a few questions:

Facilitator:

–   *How long have I been working in this department?*

Barbara in the role of Lise:

– *For 43 years.*

Facilitator:

– *When did the services first start to become computerised?*

Barbara in the role of Lise:

– *Five years ago.*

Facilitator (to group):

– *Now I invite you to ask Barbara some questions, using the 'I' form.*

A participant:

– *Can I, Lise, say that say that there was a preparatory period leading up to the introduction of the computerised system?*

Barbara in the role Lise:

– *Not as far as I am aware. In any case, no one gave me any form of preparation!*

A participant:

– *With what do I, Lise, associate computerisation?*

Barbara in the role of Lise:

– *For me, it's extremely stressful and I don't want any of it. I have no internet at home and I manage very well without it.*

A participant:

– *Have my former colleagues from that time all left by now?*

Barbara in the role of Lise:

– *Yes, there's no one else left from my generation. I'm the very last.*

A participant:

– *How do I get on with the rest of the staff?*

Barbara in the role of Lise:

– *Pffffr . . .*

Facilitator:

– *How do I see my boss, Barbara?*

Barbara in the role of Lise (laughing):

– *She drives me mad. If she thinks she can push us around like pawns on a chessboard, she's got another think coming. That's not going to work with ME. The young new recruits can take over using these machines but I have only a year to go to retirement and I just want to be left alone to get on with my job as I've always done it and know how to do it.*

A participant:

    – *Do I enjoy my work?*

Barbara in the role of Lise:

    – *Well, yes, I used to. But now I literally have to drag myself into the office each morning.*

A participant:

    – *Do I remember a point in time at which I was forced to accept a small change in MY way of working?*

Barbara:

    – *Yes, when we had to revise the document preparation procedures three years ago.*

After these questions, the facilitator initiated the phase of the work that would help Barbara come out of her role as Lise, the 'de-roling' procedure. This de-roling takes place in three phases:

- Step 1 of de-roling: what was felt while playing the role

The facilitator asked Barbara to change places with him. Then he asked her:

Facilitator:

    – *Barbara, what did you feel while playing the role of Lise?*

Barbara:

    – *In the role of Lise, I felt afraid. I felt that it was going to be a very demanding enterprise and that I wasn't sure that I was up to it.*

- Step 2 of de-roling: coming out of the role

Facilitator:

    – *Barbara, I would suggest that you stand up. Now that you are on your feet, you can stamp and rub and shake your clothes as if you were shaking off the role (the facilitator does this at the same time as Barbara). Who are you now? Tell us your name loudly and clearly!*

Barbara:

    – *BARBARA !*

The facilitator then asked Barbara to return to her seat in the group, the place where she had been sitting before being asked to take up a role.

●   Step 3 of the de-roling: what was felt in taking up the role

Facilitator to Barbara, who had returned to where she had been sitting earlier:

–   *What did it enable you to feel, Barbara, taking on the role of Lise?*

Barbara:

–   *I'm now much better aware of her difficulties, the more so in that, when I was in Lise's place, playing the role, I really did have a strong sense of how limited I was in the face of computers, it all seemed excessively complicated to me.*

The facilitator moved on to Stage 5, sharing, and now addressed the group, inviting participants to share whatever had been evoked in them by what had taken place:

Facilitator (to group):

–   *Does the experiment as it was conducted with Barbara evoke any memories, thoughts or feelings in you? Does it remind you of anything you have yourselves experienced?*

Participants:

–   *It reminds me of my experience with a colleague who used to refuse to attend staff meetings.*

–   *In my professional experience in a private company such a thing would never have happened!*

Then the facilitator came back to the question originally asked and developed in Stage 3:

Facilitator:

–   *Let us come back to our initial question: how is it possible to motivate people who ask 'what is the point?', who 'have always worked in this way' and are reluctant to move towards change of any kind?*

The facilitator proposed looking together for ways of moving forward and action strategies.

Facilitator:

- *On the basis of your own resources and experience, and to answer the question asked at the outset, what steps seem important to you to be taken in a context such as that evoked by Barbara? What ways forward, what action would you advocate or could you imagine?*

Proposals were offered by several participants:

- *Check whether every possible kind of effort has been made.*
- *At least maintain contact with the colleague.*
- *Ascertain the underlying causes of the refusal.*
- *Bear in mind that in some cases people are unwilling to attend training because they have a low level of education and are afraid.*
- *Offer empathy in relation to the person's experience while, at the same time, drawing attention to the duties and obligations attaching to work to be performed and services provided.*
- *Take a person seriously and demonstrate appreciation of their skills.*
- *Prepare for Lise's replacement by drawing up a job description that stipulates the requirement for good computer skills.*

These paths, ideas, pieces of advice, messages were written up on a chart, after which Barbara was asked to say something about where she was now:

Facilitator:

- *Barbara, you have heard the group members do some searching on your behalf. Perhaps there may even be people here who are experiencing similar problems. Now it is you who have the floor. Where are you now? What is it that is most alive for you in the here and now? What is it that seems important for you in managing this type of situation and what is your message for the group?*

It sometimes happens that participants express frustration when, in response to a question that has been asked, several possible paths have been mentioned without any immediate and operational solution having been arrived at. In such cases the facilitator will stress that the work underway is just one stage in a longer search:

Participant:

- *Yes, but we haven't found any solution to Barbara's problem!*

Facilitator:

  – *I'd like to thank you for your reaction because it enables me to say that what matters is that we have set Barbara's question in motion. And the fact of having set it in motion by means of the Empathy Circle sets us all in motion, linking up with other situations that everyone experiences in one form or another in their working life. Together, in a context of collective intelligence, we are searching, and we are experimenting here today in common.*

  – *After that, well, it's rather like throwing a pebble into the water: a series of circles forms, each larger than the other, around the point where the pebble hit the water. And the movement continues. Sometimes connections are established as a result. This work relies upon a maturation process that continues in the wake of the work that has been done here. We can ask Barbara where she is now.*

Barbara:

  – *It does me good to speak about this problem that has been really getting me down. I say to myself that it is a good idea to focus on what Lise has achieved in the course of her career (silence) . . . . For example, she's a very reliable person, and very well organised. Her organisational flair could help her to make the transition to computerised techniques in a step-by-step manner. Of course, it would be much more positive, for both of us, if I were to regard the situation in this light . . . .*

Barbara, three weeks later in another supervision session, reported to the group:

  – *I had a meeting with Lise and what surprised me was that I found myself more open towards her and the exchange seemed to me much less burdensome than I had imagined. We're not over the river yet, but she has agreed to select a colleague who would coach her. It's a small opening but we can keep our fingers crossed!*

The Empathy Circle allows an experience that is a kind of 'vertical dive' into the role of a third person, with the help of the group. The Revealing Chairs technique, which will be dealt with next, enables a more 'horizontal' exploration by means of a staging of the context.

Finding out more

There exists, as described by – among many others – the neuropsychiatrist and author Jean Michel Oughourlian, a medical imaging procedure, the PET scan, enabling identification of which zone of the brain is being stimulated in order to perform an action. The PET scan measures the activity of a neuron or a zone of the brain on the basis of the rate of glucose absorption required at one precise moment in order to function. Numerous teams of scientists are continuing work on the enigma of the mirror neurons, also referred to as empathy neurons. Their question is the following : How is this resonance, this neurological connection among persons that enables the reciprocal capture of intentions, actions and emotions, able to take place?

With relation to this research and the complexity of the neuroscientific phenomena involved, we would stress, in our own field of enquiry, the importance of the following research question:

–   *How can we create group contexts that foster empathy?*

We observe and hear feedback from participants in training sessions who, after role-taking and when they subsequently again see persons whose role they have played, realise that there has been a change. Communication has become less difficult; something unexpected is experienced with persons who had previously seemed to be at the root of a problematic situation; there is a new release of positive energy experienced as generating a small, yet significant and favourable, change in the atmosphere of the relationship.

It seems that these techniques thus activate skills, possessed by everyone, for the creation of new information, by closely attuning perception to the presence and being of another person and establishing contact through a sensitivity to relationship. It becomes therefore appropriate to consider which are the methods or techniques, regarded from this angle, that would form a basis to encourage learning in the area of empathy.

Technique 4: Revealing Chairs

How can we open up thinking by incorporating contextual elements?

With the Revealing Chairs technique, several empty chairs representing different aspects of a question and its context are placed in the meeting space. And those participants who so wish come forward to give voice to these chairs.

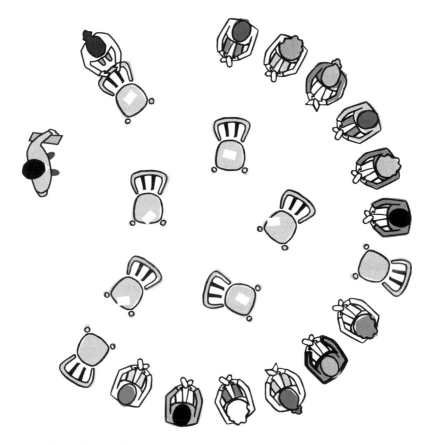

Figure 10 Revealing Chairs technique

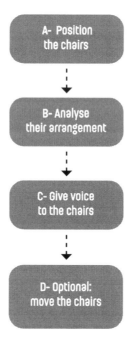

Figure 11 How to use Revealing Chairs

Use of the Revealing Chairs

This technique, like all those presented in this book, is used in the context of the ARC process described earlier. During the first stage, the safety frame is put in place. When working with the Revealing Chairs, it is highly advisable to observe all stages of the ARC process. Stage 2 is important for setting up a relationship context that will foster spontaneity and working on the move. Stage 3, the question, enables the group to be positioned in a direction that accords with its goal. The Revealing Chairs experiment comes in Stage 4, which is the action stage. Sharing in Stage 5 is essential to enable all participants, including those who did not take part in the role-playing, to become involved and express their point of view. Stage 6 is the operational fruit of the collective intelligence work: the search for new paths and action strategies.

The Revealing Chairs approach is easily linked up with the conceptual framework of systemic analysis, because it stimulates a sense of 'context'. This refers to the capacity to perceive and understand, on the relational level as well as in a more all-encompassing manner, any form of reality as a complex and interactive system.

Work with the Revealing Chairs takes place in four phases as illustrated in Figure 11:

Phase A: positioning the chairs

On the basis of the question that has just been formulated, identify the persons, entities and elements that can usefully be represented by empty chairs. The facilitator stands up and invites participants to position the chairs in relation to one another.

Facilitator to group:

– *I would suggest, if you agree, that we conduct an experiment. What are the main features that need to be taken into consideration in relation to the question that we are asking? These 'features' may be:*

- *Persons.*
- *Groups.*
- *Entities such as institutions, companies, organisations or other structures.*
- *Concepts such as values, ideas, or symbols.*

Let's go. As we identify and name these persons, groups, entities and/or concepts, we will represent them by empty chairs that we will position in our working area. We will pay attention to how we position these empty chairs in relation to each other. So as not to overburden our memories, we will stick a post-it on each chair to indicate what it represents.

During the positioning of the chairs, as we decide exactly how to place them, what distance to leave between them, or even whether to put them on top of one another, people speak to one another and already begin to create information. Each person in the group has their own vision of things:

- *Where should we put this chair?*
- *Why should it be given such a central position?*
- *I would put it in front.*

These discussions will bring to the fore similarities and differences in ways of seeing the same situation, question or project. In seeking to construct a common representation with the chairs, the group has set to work in search of a common vision.

Variant: The empty chairs may be replaced, for example, by coloured sheets of paper placed on the floor. The important thing is that people should be able to move around, to 'feel' and speak in the place of the different chairs or sheets of paper. Coloured sheets are more interesting than plain white ones because different colours stimulate the use of a sense-oriented and symbolic approach. When the group is asked to choose a colour to represent a person, a group, an entity or a concept, information will be created. What made us choose red here? Or black there? These discussions will enable the representations of each participant to come to light and be explicitly shared. For example:

- *Red for the hierarchy because they are the ones who decide.*
- *I would be more inclined to choose green because we are placing our hope in the decisions that they will take.*

Phase B: analysis of the positioning of the chairs in relation to each other

This stage consists in a 'freezing' of the picture in order to consider what it says about how the overall context is represented by the group.

Facilitator (to group):
- *I would ask you now to observe what kind of a representation you have put in place by arranging the chairs in precisely this manner. What does this arrangement evoke for you? What do you have to say about the distance or closeness between chairs? What strikes you as particularly meaningful? Is there something that you find surprising? Thinking back to your context, what comments would you make?*

Reference sheet 16 contains instructions prompting the group to react to a creation it has put in place jointly.

Phase C: letting the chairs speak

Facilitator:

– *Right now I am proposing that 'whoever so wishes' should stand up and come out here to say something on behalf of what or who is represented by one or several of these chairs. You may place your hands on the chair back and say out loud whatever it is that comes from within 'on behalf of' whatever it is that your chosen chair is representing.*

– *Do not hesitate to stand up and come behind a chair even without knowing in advance what you are going to say. You will then allow yourself to feel whatever comes to you at the time, at that precise moment. You can even close your eyes if that helps you. Each participant, after coming out here to speak, returns to their seat. You may come several times.*

> With the Revealing Chairs technique, the group as a whole is asked to contribute to the action, with each person remaining free to become involved at his or her own pace.

One constraint is announced by the facilitator:

– *Should it be the case that one of the chairs represents you personally, then you may not come to speak behind that particular chair. This ensures that everyone always takes up a role other than his or her own. This is because the purpose of the experiment is to come to see a situation from a standpoint that is different from one's own.*

There is, however, a special case within this rule: if a chair represents, rather than an individual person, a group of persons, for example the administrative staff, then it is possible, even if one belongs to this team, to come to play the role of this chair. This is because the chair represents a group rather than an individual. Insofar as the notion of group is broader and more varied than that of individual, the person who takes up this role, even if he or she is a member of the administration department, will be speaking from a position removed from his or her own personal stance: *I am speaking not on my own behalf but on behalf of a group.*

Phase D (optional): alter the position of the chairs

It is possible to ask the group, or one member of the group, to alter the position of the chairs. This phase can prove extremely rich because the movement supplies, in a non-verbal manner, indications

> Repositioning the chairs brings our senses into play.

about a change that is considered desirable. This often springs from an intuitive dimension from which spontaneous and less conscious components can create new openings.

Facilitator:

–   *Now that we have taken time for thought, what change or changes would you be inclined to make in the positioning of the chairs? Go ahead and show us.*

–   *What information is supplied by this change? What else can we say in relation to this repositioning?*

Then we come to Stage 5, the sharing phase.

Facilitator:

–   *You have taken up roles, you have observed. What has been important for you in what has happened here? What is it that struck you particularly while you were doubling the chairs and/or in your position as observer?*

The sharing phase then allows a return to the initial question that was drawn up in Stage 3 and leads into Stage 6 of the collective search for ways forward and action strategies.

Facilitator:

–   *After this experiment in which we have just taken part, let us come back to our initial question. What ways forward and action strategies would you say we might consider?*

Variant: In the situation where one person is the main protagonist affected by the initial question, the following arrangement may be proposed:

Facilitator (to the 'protagonist' participant, or the person who raised the question):

–   *I would now ask you to step back a little and not to intervene. Your colleagues, on the basis of all that has been experienced here and of their own personal experience and reference points, will together consider how to reply to your question. After that, we will ask you to speak once more.*

Several options may well have been proposed by the group. At the end of the brainstorming, the participant who momentarily moved to the back is given the final say and can explain where he is now in terms of feeling, cognitive understanding, and the possibility of finding a way forward.

Facilitator (to the participant who had been asked to 'stand back'):

–   *You helped to build the sculpture of chairs, you have played different roles and heard your colleagues play roles. What would you now like to say to conclude this working session? What is most alive for you at this moment? What will you decide to take with you? What changes would you be inclined to put in place as from tomorrow?*

Returning the chairs to their original positions is an essential component of the working session:

Facilitator:

–   *To complete this working session, we will together put the chairs back where they were before we started. I would propose that each of you should pick up a chair and, while returning it to its place, offer a closing message.*

Putting the chairs away is a form of de-roling, a ritual for concluding the proceedings and returning the chairs to their status as objects.

Points for attention

● Request the group's consent before using this technique.

● It is advisable to place a post-it or other form of label on each chair with the name of what it represents.

● Each participant may go to stand behind the chair of his or her choice provided the chair in question does not represent him or her directly. It may in some cases be considered that a group of persons does not represent one person directly and this means that a participant may go to represent a group of which he or she is a member and speak on behalf of the group rather than in a personal capacity.

● It is recommended, in order to encourage role-playing behind the chairs, that the facilitator remain standing and available, when appropriate, to accompany participants to the chair of their choice, enabling them to feel supported. The facilitator may encourage the group verbally:

–   *Would you like to give it a try?*

–   *Who's going to come forward?*

–   *It's an experiment, there can be no question of making a mistake, it's a matter of trial and error. Who would like to begin?*

● The facilitator can also be alert to non-verbal cues – a participant who appears hesitant to come forward, who is looking at the floor, or staring at the chairs, a hand looking inclined to move towards the play area – and respond to them by saying, for example:

–   *Well, come along then, I'm inviting you to come forward and try something out.*

- If people are finding it difficult to get up, for example because they are feeling shy or fearful, the facilitator may decide not to insist and, instead, to herself take on roles. She asks persons to say what they would say in the place of one or other pole represented by the empty chairs and then herself echoes from behind a chair what participants have said from their own places.

  Facilitator behind the chair representing the client:

  - *If you were to stand up to take the place of the client, what would you say?*

  Participant speaking from own chair:

  - *I would say 'we need this product right now and not one month from now'.*

  Facilitator standing behind the chair representing the client, playing the role of the client:

  - *I am the client and all I have to say to you is that we need this product right now. And not in a month!!!*

  The fact of playing the role standing behind a chair will attract the group's attention. Effects will be amplified and the experience will feed into the sharing and the search for ways forward and action strategies.

- In the methodology of the Revealing Chairs, when participants speak on behalf of the chairs, they stand behind the chairs and may place their hands on the chair back. They do not sit down on the empty chairs. This procedure enables something just less than full involvement that makes it possible to switch from one role to another without the need for de-roling.

- The facilitator may decide that persons come to take a role one by one. She may also choose to let several people express themselves simultaneously, and hold a dialogue with each other, in their chosen roles, while standing behind the empty chairs.

- When a person stands up to play a role, she may also immediately afterwards take up another role and go to stand behind one or more other chairs before returning to her place.

- Depending on the context, the facilitator may choose to himself play roles or not to do so. When the process and group dynamic demand more attention, it is advisable not to play roles, and to place the emphasis on the facilitator as an outsider (third party) guaranteeing the safety frame and the regulation of what is taking place in the group.

Illustrations

Cooperation: cooperation difficulties between departments

The facilitator is running a management training session. She begins by putting in place the safety frame, Stage 1 of the ARC process, and explains that the training session will take place in a spirit of (re)search, with the aim of co-construction.

At an early stage of the work, Mark, a middle man-ager in a public authority department, gives expression to difficulties of cooperation between his own depart-ment and other services with which it is linked. As several persons and different teams of colleagues are enmeshed in these difficulties, the facilitator's hypoth-esis is that the Revealing Chairs tool could contribute enlightenment by enabling participants to construct a common representation of this fraught context.

> Facilitator's hypothesis: to construct together a repre-sentation of the context using Revealing Chairs could be a way of viewing the situa-tion together from new and different angles.

Facilitator (to Mark):

– *How might you formulate your question?*

Mark:

– *The question could be 'How can we improve communication among depart-ments?'*

The facilitator then invites Mark to set the chairs in position and name the persons or entities that they represent. In this way, several entities are represented: the team, the colleague, the administration, the internal services and the hierarchy. The facilitator then invites those group members who so wish to stand up, go to stand behind the chair or chairs of their choice, and take on roles.

In this way, the members of the group give voice to the entities represented by the empty chairs:

Behind the empty chair representing the team:

– *I've been doing this job for only a short time. I'm highly motivated but I'm drown-ing. I'm so behind with my work and absolutely have to catch up, even if it means working overtime.*

Behind the chair of the colleague:

– *I'm desperately trying to keep everyone happy.*

Behind the chair of the external service:

– *No one knows why we still have no answer, no one knows what to expect, no one understands. And yet I really am doing all I can.*

Behind the chair of the team:

- *The telephone has been out of order for two days and no one has done anything about it.*

Behind the chair of the hierarchy:

- *I have more than enough to cope with and no time to go to see what's happening in the other departments.*

When the role-playing has come to an end, the facilitator proposes letting participants share their experiences, thoughts and observations. This is Stage 5.

- *Everyone wants to make progress.*
- *The person managing purely administrative aspects fails to understand what is at stake.*
- *It seems we are operating on quite different wavelengths.*
- *There are political repercussions.*
- *We feel oppressed.*
- *No one came to speak behind the chair representing the administration.*

The facilitator then proposed to take time to co-construct action paths and strategies.

Various paths were proposed:

- *Imagine what kind of document might be used to ensure that requests made by one department to another were placed on official record.*
- *Move over to direct word-of-mouth communication rather than emails.*
- *Sit the persons concerned around a table.*
- *Come to an agreement with the hierarchy.*
- *Create alliances.*

At the end of the brainstorming session, Mark said:

- *Thanks to the fact that we were able to represent the situation in visual form, I already feel much less alone. The Revealing Chairs technique helped me to visualise our environment including the different persons affected by the com-*

munication problem. I will take up this analysis in a meeting. And I will take inspiration from our work to suggest to my team that together we draw up a chart to represent our situation. In this way, we'll be able to name the different persons and groups involved and see them represented on a sheet of paper. I see this as a way forward for dealing with the problem in our team. Thank you.

Marketing: promoting and disseminating a new project

The facilitator is accompanying development of the project presented by Carola who is in charge of the 'internet site'. After a year of intensive work, the project consists in promoting and presenting to citizens a new interactive internet site, as well as its access app, in the hope of making it into a 'must have' for all smartphones. This website would give people access to a tremendous amount of useful information in the fields in question.

Carola began by pointing out that the partners of this project were at the same time the competitors. She suggested that a meeting among all parties, internal and external, could help to create a sense of belonging and to develop new ways of working together.

Accompanied by the facilitator, the twelve colleagues involved – internal and external partners – have come together for a brainstorming session, the explicit purpose of which is to strengthen the team and develop new strategic directions for promoting the internet site.

The facilitator organised the work in several stages:

Stage 1 of the ARC process, setting up the safety frame. The five working rules were stated: spontaneity, freedom, 'bring-back', discretion, punctuality.

Stage 2 of the ARC process, start-up:

–   *Working on factors of connection.* Participants walked around in the meeting room and, at a signal from the facilitator, formed sub-groups, ensuring that these included members of the different teams. The facilitator suggested that they exchange some ideas on 'factors of connection in relation to the project underway'. In other words, how did each of them envisage the project? What would they like to say about it? What points of view and experiences did they share?

–   *Work on competences.* The facilitator, with the group, drew up an inventory of the skills that had already been deployed in order to bring this internet site into existence, on the part of Carola's own team as well as on that of the partner/competitors. She listed all these skills on a board where they could be seen by everyone.

During the discussion that preceded the group work, Carola had formulated her question (and her request) as follows:

– *'How can we maximise the launching of this internet site?'*

The facilitator posed this question in the group setting and suggested working on it using an action method.

To represent the complexity inherent in the question, the facilitator put forward the hypothesis that the Revealing Chairs would enable participants to build up a common representation, to express their differences and reservations, to stand back from the subject, to put into words their own specific way of seeing things. The outcome of this work process could be an increase in cohesion.

To initiate Stage 4 of the action, the facilitator proposed that participants place in the centre of the room a number of empty chairs, each of which would represent one aspect of the issues arising in relation to promotion of the internet site.

Empty chairs were thus arranged in the central part of the meeting area, representing different stakeholders: citizens, the marketing director, management, the internal team, the external partners, the competitors, the internet site.

Choices about where and how to position and arrange the chairs allowed participants' varying ways of seeing to emerge.

> Facilitator's hypothesis: the revealing chairs would enable each participant to give expression to his or her own way of envisaging the project. This process could help to move forward towards a shared representation, thereby enhancing cohesion.

Participants:

– *I would see the marketing chair placed right in the centre because all the financial decisions that affect dissemination are in their hands.*

– *Oh no, that's not at all how I see it. I would place that chair somewhere further back, because the most central concern here is citizens and finding ways of getting them interested and involved.*

– *Ah . . . all right, then let's try to place it in a central position, just slightly back from the citizen.*

The group then received the following instruction:

Facilitator:

> – *Anyone who so wishes should go to stand behind the chair of his or her choice and say something on behalf of whoever or whatever it is that this chair represents. There's just one special rule: no one may go to stand behind the chair that represents him or herself in person.*

> *If one of you chooses, for example, to come to speak behind the marketing director's chair, he or she will say something of relevance to what the marketing director might be experiencing, what he might think or say. It is a question, in other words, of always moving away from one's own centre, standing back, seeing things from a different angle.*

At this point participants proceeded to 'give voice', in the manner described by the facilitator, to the empty chairs.

Behind the 'citizen' chair:

> – *If I discover that I like this site, then I'll be inclined to tell other people about it.*

Behind the marketing director's chair:

> – *What we mustn't forget is that I have a fixed budget.*

Behind the project development group chair:

> – *We've devoted so many hours of hard work to this project that I would really like to see it take off.*

Behind the external partners' chair:

> – *The success of this project is extremely important for us because it will broaden our market!*

Behind the internet site chair:

> – *I'm actually quite fragile. I do have a structure but I could be made much more robust and personalised.*

Behind the competitors' chair:

> – *We're already one step further on than you are.*

The facilitator then invited participants to say something about their experience of the group experiment that had just taken place. Some comments were as follows:

Safety frame — Start up — Question — Action — Sharing — Strategy ➡

     –   *It turns out that the team actually has quite limited room for manoeuvre.*

     –   *The management is beginning to have some doubts. What can we do to convince them?*

     –   *The clients are pretty demanding and so we're going to need some solid arguments.*

     –   *It's as if synergy were lacking because there are so many aspects that lie beyond our control. We are faced with the need to convince the marketing department of the need to make more funds available.*

     –   *I was very struck to hear Luigi, in the role of the citizen, and hence the potential consumer, mention the inclination to tell others about the interest and benefits of the site.*

The facilitator, through the comments from participants, expressed the hypothesis of an implicit rule present in the group which might be translated as 'success is a matter of finding convincing arguments'. Indeed, he had observed that participants often spoke of 'putting forward solid arguments' or 'getting them to understand that'.

With this hypothesis in mind, the facilitator reminded the group what the initial question had been:

     –   *'How can we maximise the launching of the internet site?'*

The process had now reached Stage 6, namely, the search for ways forward and action strategies.

In the wake of the work with the Revealing Chairs, several participants returned to Luigi's role-playing when, from behind the citizen's chair, he had referred to the satisfied consumer who would be keen to share his enthusiasm with others.

On the basis of this role-playing, an idea emerged, namely that of inviting consumers to come to speak on the radio!

Rather than convincing through the use of argument, the idea would be to open up a space in which members of the public could have a say.

The facilitator connected what was happening with his hypothesis. If an implicit rule was in force in the group, and if this rule could be expressed in terms of 'success is a matter of finding convincing arguments', then the idea of inviting consumers to come to share their ideas and responses in public would be a way of activating a dynamic of a different kind than that of 'convincing'.

Facilitator:

     –   *By latching on to the idea of bringing consumers in to come to say something about their personal experience, you are introducing change. It is no longer a question of putting in place convincing advertising campaigns but of listening to consumers and taking the risk of doing this directly on the air. How will it be for you to experience this new way of doing things?*

Participant:

– *As our site is interactive, this way of getting the public to come to speak directly about their experience would be quite compatible with our approach and the internet site itself. At the same time, we are taking a risk, because we won't have any control over what the consumers might say.*

In the light of our explanation in Part 2 of this book, and of Key 5, the facilitator's work here entailed use of a systemic reading grid, through the demonstration of sensitivity to the question of implicit rules. If the implicit rule is that 'success is a matter of finding convincing arguments', then increasing the number of advertising campaigns would be to 'do more of the same thing' and hence remaining within a type 1 change.

By contrast, inviting people to come to speak on a radio programme would entail a different kind of advertising dynamic. It would no longer be a question of *convincing* but rather of *listening*. The change here is a change of type, a change in the very nature and quality of change!

As from the point when people position themselves differently in relation to the implicit rule 'success is a matter of finding convincing arguments', it may be that a new field for action will open up and that, in this way, the chances of sensitising and influencing potential consumers will be enhanced.

As the facilitator thinks through all these aspects and questions in his inner mind, he brings into play the particular research dynamic that is a hallmark of his work. He begins by observing, goes on to formulate hypotheses, chooses a mode of intervention in the light of these hypotheses, carefully observes its effects in action, and so the process goes on.

The group creativity and innovative ideas that emerge from this work demonstrate to what extent the systemic approach and its characteristic references are able to enrich and stimulate change through the use of the Revealing Chairs, and of action techniques in general.

To complete this particular work, the facilitator proposed to participants that they form sub-groups and search together for ways forward and action strategies along three priority axes:

- The internal communication axis.
- The external communication axis.
- The internet site promotion axis.

Ideas were collected on post-its and displayed on a support visible to all. They were read out to the group as a whole by a representative of each of the sub-groups. These ideas would then be able to be used by the persons responsible for promotion of the website.

In addition to the ideas, new paths and action strategies that emerged from collective intelligence, the Revealing Chairs experiment here proved to be way of enabling the various partners to take the time to perceive and formulate the nature and dimensions of the project in all its complexity and to create a common language. As a result of this experience, several bridges were subsequently built among the different protagonists and interaction among the parties was stepped up in a constructive way.

Finding out more

The effort to 'link up with what has not yet been put into words', the transition from the implicit to the explicit, is a process central also to other methodological approaches. One of these is the *Systemic Organisation Constellations*, developed in the 2000s by, among others, the German systemic psychiatrist and psychotherapist Gunthard Weber.

More recently, two authors who have worked as both psychodramatists and constellators, Ronald Anderson and Karen Carnabucci, have sought to integrate the practice of psychodrama with that of constellations in their book *Integrating psychodrama and systemic constellation work* (2012).

In the constellations framework, a client places, in what is called the 'energy field or knowledge field', one or more persons, placing a hand on their shoulder. When they have been thus positioned, the persons are invited to take whatever time they need to allow the resurfacing within themselves of sensations, emotions, thoughts or desires of movement, in an attitude of openness and non-intentional perception, also known as 'floating attention'.

Bridges are to be explored and we believe that a dialogue among professionals favouring and trained in different approaches is a way of viewing these various approaches from a new angle, enriching them and potentially enabling them to evolve in new directions.

Technique 5: Analogical Detours

How can we move away from our habitual ways of thinking and come back to them via a creative detour?

Analogical Detours technique is made up of several sub-techniques, such as Metaphors, Shapes and Colours, Symbolic Objects and Similar-sounding Words, that enable participants to gain some distance or detachment without necessarily entailing role-playing but rather by making use of the analogical and symbolic dimensions.

Figure 12 Analogical Detours

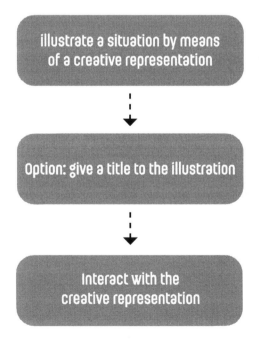

Figure 13 How to use Analogical Detour

Using Analogical Detours

Just like the already described techniques of Doubling, Empty Chair, Empathy Circle and Revealing Chairs, the Analogical Detours can enable a same situation to be regarded from different angles. This technique, which encompasses a range of sub-techniques, differs from the others in that here the change in the angle of vision can be achieved by means of a creative illustration that does not, in the first instance, entail role-playing.

> The Analogical Detours will enable a same situation to be viewed from a different angle, by means of a creative illustration.

Each facilitator, in his or her own work, can create analogical detours using the voice, objects found in nature, paint, special cards, etc.

The Analogical Detour can be used in a 'spontaneous version' or a 'sequential version'.

Spontaneous version

In the spontaneous version, either a metaphor may be spontaneously introduced in the course of discussion, or one or more people can be asked to produce a 'drawing' or 'illustration' of whatever it is they are talking about.

Sequential version

In the sequential version, a specific period of time can be set aside for a piece of work with Analogical Detour in the form of an experiment or exercise.

> Each facilitator can create his or her analogical detours in relation to the references and methodologies with which s/he is familiar.

Through the detours created by analogies, participants can exploit their capacity for associating a real situation with more metaphorical elements. This is achieved by experimentation with a form of 'detour through symbols' that makes use of creative thinking. In this way, participants are enabled to say something about their experience without revealing it in any more detail than they wish or feel to be appropriate. Through recourse to the imagination, some experience takes on a form that is simultaneously auditory and visual. Images include dimensions that resonate with the senses, the emotions, the unconscious, and intuition. The symbolic space thus created and opened up encompasses the whole group.

Every time that use is made of an analogical detour, in each creative illustration or metaphor, it is possible to consider a process, a number of stages, and a dynamic to be decoded. Such decoding facilitates movement beyond the original question, contributing, in addition, answers to other questions as yet unformulated or only hazily envisaged.

It is to be borne in mind that each analogical detour has its own dynamic, active process, and stages, all of which are to be decoded.

When using the Analogical Detour, there will be less differentiation between Stages 5 (sharing) and 6 (strategies) of the ARC process. The facilitator will, at one and the same time, support the group in calling up the creative illustration, encourage sharing, and stimulate the search for ways forward and action strategies. The ways forward will take definite shape, gradually, through a process of sharing and an interweaving of the information and associations that will circulate around the creative illustration.

Points for attention

- As with every action technique, it is important to enquire whether the persons present agree to work together using the chosen technique.

- To enable the analogical detours to operate effectively, the ARC process is to be kept in mind and used to facilitate a staged process that will stimulate collective intelligence.

(i) Metaphors

Participants create one or more metaphor(s) that illustrate the situation under discussion. The experience of creating metaphors can take place individually, in subgroups, or in a broader group.

The metaphor allows illustration of a question or situation by the use of symbols, colours, images and sensations. It can also take the form of a proverb, a scenario, a link with a film, a song, a painting, etc.

David's work overload

The facilitator, in the context of a communication training session, is working on situations arising 'in the field'. David, who works in a bank, describes a difficulty he is experiencing in his job:

David:

– *I simply do not have the resources to cope with the situations that arise. I am given no help and feel increasingly left to my own devices in the face of an ever growing mountain of work.*

Facilitator (to David):

– *How would you formulate your question more precisely?*

David:

– *'How can I create some space?'*

The facilitator expresses the hypothesis that a detour via metaphors could help David to feel less stuck in an impossible situation and to connect up with new resources. What is more, in the course of this training session, while dealing with an earlier situation, the group has already made use of role-playing. In this particular context, therefore, the use of metaphors as an action method represents a way of varying the approaches, mobilising the group as a whole and allowing a detour via symbolic dimensions without recourse to role-playing.

Facilitator's hypothesis: the work with metaphors would enable creation of information which could then be used as a resource for achieving progress in relation to the initial question.

Facilitator (to group):

– *In relation to the problem broached by David, I would like you to form sub-groups. You have three minutes to find a metaphor, an image that could, in your view, illustrate the situation in which David currently finds himself.*

Facilitator (to groups as they search for metaphors):

– *You have one minute 30 seconds left to find your metaphor!*

The time limit stimulates creativity, encouraging people to come up quickly with a spontaneous idea without thinking too hard. The sub-groups then share the metaphors they have created with the broader group:

– *It's like being shut up in a fortress in search of contact with the world beyond.*

– *It's like being in the middle of a swimming pool and not knowing how to swim.*

- *It's like being in a labyrinth of mirrors.*
- *It's like being in the middle of a desert, all alone in the desert.*

The facilitator encourages the group to react to the metaphors that have been created, inviting participants, at the same time, to share (Stage 5) and to seek ways forward and action strategies (Stage 6).

Facilitator (to group):

- *How is someone going to create an opening inside a fortress? Or in a labyrinth of mirrors? What can you do to save yourself if you are in a swimming pool and don't know how to swim? Or alone in the middle of the desert? How can these images be linked up with any situations that you have already experienced? What strategies did you adopt when such difficulties arose?*

David comes to see that, in all the metaphors and in the exchange that ensued, it was a question of needing help and of finding a way of calling for it. At the end of the work he put his thoughts into words as follows:

David

- *I felt almost guilty for being unable to cope, as if I lacked the requisite skills, but now I'm telling myself that I just can't go on like this. The problem is that I have a tendency to compensate, to work even harder, and to want to do everything to ensure that the machine runs smoothly. But if I go on like this, I'm the machine that will break down (laugh). I can see my limits more clearly and realise that I need to stop compensating in this way.*

(ii)   Shapes and Colours

> This Shapes and Colours technique requires the availability of pencils and crayons or felt-tipped pens. Participants, sub-groups, or groups, will illustrate the situation in question on a large sheet of paper, using different shapes, symbols and colours.

For this technique it is frequently preferable to use terms such as 'creative illustration', 'graphical representation', use of 'shapes and colours', rather than 'drawing' which can sometimes be a frightening notion for participants because of the suggestion that one needs to 'know how to draw'. Here the 'graphical representation' is experimental and is one component of a search, abstracting from any aesthetic consideration.

Harry who feels 'stuck' in his job

> Facilitator's hypothesis: working with Shapes and Colours could be a way to help this head of department to set aside his habitual way of thinking and, in so doing, discover some mental space in which to seek solutions.

The facilitator is coaching a head of department, Harry, who is experiencing a difficult time in the company for which he works. After explaining his situation to the facilitator, Harry falls silent, hoping for some kind of a response, some words that would open up the possibility of a way forward. The facilitator's hypothesis is that the whole subject could be best approached from a new angle.

To Harry's astonishment, the facilitator hands him a sheet of paper and pencil and says:

– *How could the situation you describe be illustrated on this sheet?*

Harry:

– *I'm no good at drawing . . . . And in any case . . . how is it going to help?*

Facilitator:

– *Just go ahead, we'll see what happens, it's not a question of drawing but of illustrating your experience, your questions, your feelings. We're taking time for an experiment, using a creative illustration, as a way of trying to understand your situation and seek ways forward. Is that all right?*

> There is no need to be 'good at drawing' in order to produce this kind of spontaneous creative representation.

In this way, the facilitator encourages Harry to think in a different way, to take a detour via the 'right brain'. It is important that, before the process goes ahead, the facilitator should request Harry's permission. Harry, having agreed, begins to 'represent' his situation on a sheet of paper.

The next stage is to decode what has just been produced. The facilitator asks some questions, invites sharing, and, little by little, accompanies Harry towards a search for ways forward and action strategies.

Facilitator:

- *If we were just to fantasise and make associations, without thinking too hard, what is it that you might see in the graphic representation you have just produced?*

Harry:

- *A concrete block and a boating knot.*

Facilitator:

- *What does that tell us about your present situation?*

Harry:

- *I'm stuck, there are some knots to be undone. These knots have been building up for years.*

Facilitator:

- *How do you undo a boating knot? Is it a question of finding the part most likely to 'give'? What might this part be in your situation?*

Harry:

- *Your asking that question reminds me of how well I used to get on with my colleague Andrew a couple of years ago. He really helped me a lot.*

The facilitator draws up with Harry some links between his professional context, his representation on paper, and the dynamic of the metaphor of the boating knot. This exchange serves to establish a new 'reading grid' able to be superposed on the initial question.

In systemic terms, after hearing some details of Harry's professional context, the facilitator's hypothesis was that he felt bound by an implicit rule that governed behaviour in the company in which he worked. This rule could be stated as follows: 'to be professional is to *go it alone*'.

In referring to his former colleague Andrew, Harry had shifted his position in relation to this implicit rule. Accordingly, he began to consider asking for help and seeking to work together with others rather than stepping up his efforts to 'go it alone'. Had Harry embarked on the path of ever stronger determination to go it alone, he would have been placing himself in a type 1 change situation, i.e. one that consists in focussing one's efforts on persisting with ever greater determination along the same path.

In this instance, thanks to the use of the Analogical Detour, to the decoding of the graphical representation and the metaphor of the boating knot, the change that took place – with the facilitator's encouragement – was a change 'in the mode of change', and this we refer to as a type 2 change. Suddenly Harry came to realise that a way out of his difficulty was to ask for help. The facilitator concluded this working session with Harry by tackling the question of how he would put into practice his decision to no longer 'go it alone' in a working environment where an unwritten rule required this form of behaviour on the part of its employees.

In this case, thanks to the use of arrows, bubbles, symbols, colours, drawings, the route of graphical representation had enabled a middle manager to gain some distance from a professional situation that he had begun by describing as unbearable and yet inevitable. The intense focus on the boating knot enabled, at the very least, some space to be opened up for thinking through the situation and putting it into words.

Innovation: a group of workers wanting to innovate

The facilitator is supervising a team that is seeking to innovate, in terms of both diversifying activities and improving its internal operation.

During the start-up (Stage 2) the facilitator suggested that participants sit in a semi-circle without a table. He invited them to speak about their history and about how they would like to see their project develop over the coming years.

The initial question was formulated by the group as follows:

– *What new fields of application could enable us to innovate and find new ways of working?*

The facilitator's hypothesis was that, for this particular task calling for collective intelligence, it would be worth experimenting with the potential offered by work in the more symbolic or implicit dimensions.

Facilitator's hypothesis: requesting two participants to represent the situation on a chart would enable the emergence of information important for unleashing innovation.

The facilitator proposed the following methodological arrangement: two members of the group were invited to move some distance away from the others. The two of them were to work with their backs to the group so that the others would not be able to see what they were creating.

Facilitator (to group):

– *We are going to exchange ideas about what innovations might be feasible in your workplace. At the same time, while overhearing what we are saying, two members of the group will produce a graphical representation of what they make of our discussion. They will produce their representation each in their own way, using materials and colours of their choice.*

Imelda and Kate volunteered to make the creative representations. They moved some distance away and settled down with their backs to the group. They decided to work on the floor to produce panels. While their colleagues were discussing the prospects for innovation, Imelda and Kate would 'draw' spontaneously, each of them on a large empty sheet of paper or flipchart.

A range of topics were taken up and discussed by the group: how to set the project up and how it might develop; difficulties likely to be encountered; the dynamic within the team; potential new clients, competition; a pilot project for evaluation; new ideas, etc.

During this time, Imelda and Kate were absorbed, in silence, in the creation of their panels, present simultaneously to what was being said and to what they were setting down on paper.

After about a quarter of an hour, Imelda and Kate were asked to place their panels in the centre of the circle, on the floor, so that each member of the group could silently contemplate and take them in. Working on the floor, or at least the act of placing a creation at a certain moment on the ground, is a radical departure from the usual adult posture of working at a desk or table and a way of returning to the 'trace' on the ground with its primitive and archaic associations that restores a connection with the earth.

Facilitator (to group):

– *I would now suggest that you stand up and gather in a circle around the creations. We will then walk silently all together around them to enable us to observe them and take them in. After that, you can share your observations with Imelda and Kate, telling them what strikes you particularly, what you find meaningful, what links or similarities you notice between the two panels, and so forth.*

The facilitator then questioned the team about the creative representations and the metaphors that they contained, thereby stimulating exploration of the dynamic present in the metaphors. He invited participants to share their comments and to create links with the initial question. From this interweaving of the information in circulation, a set of possible ways forward and action strategies gradually emerged.

Facilitator:

– *Allow yourselves to share the images that come to you, give free rein to your creativity, your associations, your fantasy, your imagination. What do you see?*

One participant, Mona, shared an image that she associated with one of the panels:

- *In this drawing on the left I see a snake-like shape and it looks as if a snake were trying to find a way through a labyrinth enclosed by walls.*

Facilitator:

- *Does Mona's image mean anything to you?*

Participant:

- *This image of walls makes me think that we are so constrained by deadlines that it's impossible for us to produce work that is qualitatively valuable.*

Another participant:

- *Making our team more snake-like might be, for example, to overcome the language barrier and make our services available also in other languages.*

Another participant:

- *Why not create a new pilot project in Spanish?*

Another participant:

- *To be in a position to innovate, we should perhaps find a different way of working together . . . . We could introduce a brainstorming session at the beginning of our team meetings.*

The facilitator subsequently learned that, regularly, at their team meetings, the snake metaphor reappeared, creating openings that enabled team members to display greater flexibility and to come up with some bold ideas. This metaphor of the snake and the analogical detour helped this particular group of workers to create and develop a common language.

(iii)   Symbolic Objects

> For the Symbolic Objects, each facilitator can assemble a collection of varied objects that can subsequently be made available to groups as props for representing a situation in all its complexity.

The merging of two nurseries

The facilitator is supervising a session designed to accompany change with two groups of employees that are about to be merged. The staff in question currently work in two nurseries operating as separate units on different sites but which, in the near future, are to be brought together and merged into a single unit on the same site.

Each of the two nurseries is currently organised according to different principles. One is run on the basis of sections organised by age such that, when children move from one section to another, they are cared for by different staff. The other is run on the basis of continuity of care; infants are looked after by the same carers from when they arrive at the nursery until they leave it to enter school. Apart from these differences in the organisation of care, the two nurseries operate on the basis of different 'cultures', different codes and habits. Each of them, after all, has its separate history.

The head of the nursery has called in a facilitator, having realised that this imminent change will require organisational adjustment, and observed that the prospect of the changes in store is already a matter of fear and concern for her staff. The purpose of the work with the facilitator is to bring together the two groups of staff and to allow time for all to express whatever they may be feeling and to take part in the co-construction, through a process of collective intelligence, of the transition to a single nursery.

In Stage 1 of the ARC process the facilitator begins by putting in place the safety frame. Moving on to Stage 2, he proposes a start-up session during which participants move around the meeting area, gain awareness of their bodies, set in motion their energies, and get to know each other.

Facilitator

- *Let's walk around the room. We can feel the contact between our feet and the floor. Let's continue walking. Now let's pay attention to hearing our breathing. What is our breath doing right now? Now we are going to establish contact, in silence, by looking at the persons passing close to us. Let's once again feel the contact of our feet with the floor. Now we will create contact with one other person and this time we will say something. And then we continue walking around, and we can say something to someone else.*

After this warming-up exercise, the facilitator proposed to participants the technique of the Spectrogram. He asked them to come to position themselves along an imaginary diagonal line – stretching right across the room – in accordance with one specific criterion, namely, their seniority in terms of years worked. One end of the line was to represent the longest-serving staff member and the other end the most recently recruited.

The facilitator's hypothesis was that working in this way on the basis of one specific aspect of shared experience would be a means of strengthening forms of connection other than the fact of belonging to one nursery or the other.

Once participants had positioned themselves along this imaginary line, the facilitator asked them to form groups of four or five persons each. In this way all participants found themselves grouped together with colleagues or future colleagues with a similar number of years of work experience to their own.

Facilitator:

> – *Now that you are in small groups, begin to consider and to talk about any connections that you might share. You can speak about anything you wish.*

After about ten minutes, the facilitator continued:

> – *Now I would like to ask you to formulate a message that you would like to address to the other groups. This will be the specific message from your group.*

Each group prepared its message and the facilitator allowed time for each message to be spoken aloud to all the others. The 'oldest' thus addressed a message in their capacity as long-serving staff and no longer necessarily on the basis of which of the two nurseries they had worked in. The 'new' staff would also have something important to say stemming from their 'fresher' impressions. In this way, the facilitator strengthened new connections among participants and encouraged circulation of speech.

> Facilitator's hypothesis: encouraging people to mix and to collaborate on creations connected with the merging of the two nurseries would be a means of developing cohesion.

The facilitator then proposed a session with symbolic objects, on the basis of the hypothesis that choosing and manipulating objects to create panels together would stimulate even more connections among people and help them to create a common language.

Facilitator:

> – *Now I would ask you to divide up into small mixed groups of four persons, making sure that each sub-group contains persons belonging to each of the two nurseries. My proposal is to invite you to create an installation illustrating the factors of constraint and the windows of opportunity present in this merger process. You may use, for this purpose, any of the objects available on the table, placing them on a large sheet of paper as a support. You have twenty minutes to create your installation. When you have finished, I would like you to give a title to what you have made and to write this title on your sheet of paper.*

Participants formed groups and went to collect their materials. They settled down to work, talk and create together, with the support – in this case, large sheets on which participants positioned the objects – representing the safe space. Such a support ensures credibility for whatever it is that the person/group decides to build. It also enables objects to be 'invested' with a role and subsequently 'divested' of the role. At the end of the work, the act of removing the objects from their support enables them to be restored to their original status as objects, and this ritual forms part of the de-roling of the objects.

After twenty minutes have passed, the facilitator asked all participants to travel around the installations, in silence, observing them carefully and taking in the arrangements and their constituents.

Wide-ranging titles were given to the installations:

- 'Change in all its splendour'
- 'Let's do more than we thought ourselves capable of!'
- 'In union lies strength!'
- 'Nursery in wonderland'
- 'Hand in hand together'
- 'Star of life'

In speaking to and prompting the group, the facilitator had opted for a detour rather than a direct mode of approach. He invited participants to express their reactions, first of all, to one of the other creations, rather than their own. Then he asked them to establish connections among the different creative representations. And finally, at the end, members of the sub-groups were invited to say something about their own installations.

Facilitator (to participants who had returned to their places):

- *What features struck you particularly in the installations created by the other groups? What connections are you able to discern among the different panels?*
- *Now that you have shared your observations, would you like to add some comments about your own installations?*

Participants' comments included the following:

- *We see some frightening insects represented in several panels.*
- *We see the idea of building something using a rope chain and pieces of wood.*
- *The presence of scissors makes it seem that there may be something needing cutting.*
- *There is a path, but it is winding in places.*
- *In all the panels, an important constituent is attention to the spatial element.*

The facilitator continued to question the group and, at the same time, to maintain the experience of sharing and establishing links with the changes that would take place after the merger between the two nurseries. On the basis of these exchanges, a common language continued to take shape and new paths emerged.

Facilitator:

- *And now, to what points must particular attention be paid in the process of merging these two nurseries?*

Participants:

- *We are in need of reassurance, and the children too need to feel the adults solidly behind them in this process of change.*

- *Could we perhaps imagine some kind of adjustment process? What about arranging for the children to be allowed to come to visit their new environment in advance?*

- *It's definitely in our interest to prepare the parents, to explain to them what is going to happen, perhaps at a special information session?*

- *If we ourselves were able to feel less overwhelmed by the prospect of change, then we would be able to play with the children, read books to them about the experience of moving, carrying them with us and finding our way into their world by means of games.*

- *How can we put some kind of structure in place that will facilitate constructive communication among ourselves?*

- *Could we have 'one delegate per team'?*

Positive ideas thus emerged of paths that would help this merger between the two nurseries to take place in as smooth a manner as possible. Participants said that they felt relieved and reassured at the outcome of the session and that it had been a pleasure for them to come together and get to know one other in this way. The director said she felt less isolated in her task of overseeing this tremendous change. It seemed that the experience had fuelled a process of instilling resilience into the staff in general, strengthening their capacity to face up to and contribute their efforts to the success of such a difficult change.

At the end of this day-long session a project proposal was devised: to set up a working group consisting of persons representing all departments and services from both nurseries. The group's task would be to devise ways of accompanying change, taking account of all the thoughts, feelings, ideas and experiences that had been voiced and discussed in the course of the day.

(iv) Similar-sounding Words

The Similar-sounding Words was created by Chantal Nève-Hanquet. Similar-sounding words are written texts, drafted on the basis of words that illustrate a situation and that are then linked up with other words ending with a similar sound. These texts are used as an analogy to move forward with a question.

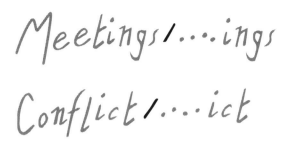

Figure 14 Similar-sounding Words

Nancy in the face of change

The facilitator is coaching a group of departmental heads. He is working on the basis of a situation from the field presented by Nancy, the head of a team of social workers.

Nancy:

— *I'm concerned at the current turn of developments in relation to the project. People find the meetings tiresome and boring. There are many complaints, with colleagues saying that what they are being asked to do feels quite alien to them. I notice inertia, a reluctance to participate, a tendency towards systematic refusal. It's getting ever more difficult. I myself really dread having to attend these meetings.*

Facilitator:

— *How would you formulate your question?*

Nancy:

— *The question would be 'how can we inspire more enthusiasm among colleagues for the work we are doing?'*

The facilitator's hypothesis was that the Similar-Sounding Words technique might well, in this particular case, prove appropriate for stimulating new paths.

> Facilitator's hypothesis: Similar-sounding Words by getting the group as a whole to focus on Nancy's question, could enable some well-worn paths to be abandoned and open up space for new approaches to work.

The work was conducted in six phases:

Phase A: associate a first word

Facilitator:

– *In your own mind, find a word that comes to you in association with what you have just heard. This first word will not be shared with the rest of the group.*

Phase B: associate a second, similar-sounding, word

Facilitator:

– *Now that you have associated a first word, I would ask you to find another word that rhymes with the first word, one that ends with the same sound.*

Phase C: compose a written text

The words chosen by the group were as follows: 'heaviness', 'goodwill', 'surpass', 'innovative', 'laughable', 'trembling', 'wish', 'paperwork', 'basket', 'birth', 'beach', 'end', 'power'. The facilitator wrote all these words on a large sheet of paper visible to everyone. The participants, divided into groups of three, composed texts containing all these words.

Phase D: read each of the texts aloud

Each group read out its jointly composed text, slowly, standing up in some cases, in order to create a theatrical effect and thereby contribute a playful as well as a dramatic note to the proceedings.

Phase E: choose a text

Nancy was at this point asked to choose, among the different stories created by the groups, the one that 'spoke' to her most, that she found to be particularly 'alive' for her, in relation to her initial question and the situation she had brought to the group.

This is the text chosen by Nancy:

Once upon a time there was a lady who, from *birth*, harboured the *wish* to display constant *goodwill*. She had always *surpassed* herself and today found herself playing a role in which she had to wield *power* without ever giving way to a *tremble*. Every day she experienced the *heaviness* of having to deal with the *paperwork*. There was no *end* to it, and no room whatsoever in this structure for anything *innovative*. The lady felt hemmed in as if she were living in a *basket*. The tasks she was striving to perform seemed *laughable* to her colleagues. And yet today was such a fine day on which to go to the *beach*'.

Phase F: ask questions, stimulate sharing and the search for ways forward and action paths

On the basis of this story, the facilitator stimulated the group to make connections. He reminded them of the initial question, stimulated analogies and creative thinking. At the same time, he prompted the group, inviting participants to share their responses. And this process gave rise to some possible ways of moving forwards.

Facilitator (to group):

- *What connections can you find between this story and Nancy's initial question which was 'how can we inspire more enthusiasm among colleagues for the work we are doing?'*

Participants had this to say:

- *This project is like having a heavy burden to carry!*
- *We might perhaps think about how the team members could be enabled to feel a bit more as if they were 'on the beach', to find ways of relaxing, feeling more comfortable, even enjoying themselves.*
- *This story gives us the trembles, it's as if people were feeling afraid. Of what?*
- *I (Nancy) feel completely at home in this story. There could be no better way of expressing what I am going through. And I'd so like to be able to disappear . . . to go off to the beach! (laughing)*

Ways forward and action strategies emerged:

- *Allow people to be actors in the project, granting them a margin of creativity.*
- *Organise a teambuilding session, perhaps in the form of an out-of-office activity.*
- *Allow time for each colleague to put into words his or her current thoughts and feelings in relation to the project.*
- *Create a climate of co-construction.*

A month later, Nancy explained that she had surprised herself by sharing her concerns with her colleagues in the workplace and had been bold enough to say something about her own doubts and discouragement. In the wake of this more open stance on her part, some of her colleagues had also spoken about their feelings of revolt in relation to current developments in the project.

'We have partly burst the abscess', she explained. 'The fact that we have found a way of speaking more naturally and opening up among ourselves within the team – and this was far from easy – has enabled a little bit of space to be opened up for us to think together about what we are trying to do in our work'. Taking up the 'beach' idea, Nancy had decided that the next meeting should be held in more pleasant surroundings!

Finding out more

The four ANALOGICAL DETOURS presented here offer routes into a fluid working session making use of one or other action method. The facilitator may, for example, have recourse to graphical representations, images, symbolic objects, or written texts, before progressing to a more extended form of work. The following would be just some of many possible examples:

- 'Giving voice to . . .': speaking on behalf of whatever is represented by one or more of the object(s), card(s), 'drawing(s)' that have been used in the initial stage of creative representation
- Role-playing: moving around and playing roles that bear some relation to the elements of the creative representation
- REVEALING CHAIRS: setting out chairs (or sheets of paper or objects) that represent elements of the creative representation and coming to stand behind these chairs, either to give them voice or, silently, to sense what is going on.

Each of these action processes fits into the ARC process. All are followed by the stages of sharing and search for ways forward and action strategies.

Frequently, even after chairs, objects, cards, and so forth, have been returned to their original positions, the participants, when speaking once again about the situation under discussion, point to the place where those objects had earlier stood. The same thing happens in work based on a metaphor. The metaphor in question is sometimes subsequently raised in a team meeting, by one person or another, in support of a point or a proposal, and this can happen even if several weeks have passed since the metaphor was first used.

In this way, the collective representation created using chairs, metaphors or some other creative tool, strengthens cohesion, helps to create a common language, and assists in co-constructing the group's aim or purpose.

With the action techniques, the participants who have been 'set in motion' undergo real practical experience of 'give and take', for example through role-taking, metaphor, or symbolic objects: taking up a role while standing behind an empty chair to work on a question raised by another group member is to *give* something to this person; to look at a drawing or diagram produced by two group members is to *receive* their creation.

This exchange will help each participant to find a place in the group. And the facilitator, by referring to this process as 'give and take', reinforces the legitimacy and skills of each group member.

As we observed in the different examples, another effect of working with the action techniques is to increase visibility of the group's 'unspoken' elements. When the implicit rules in operation in the system are enabled to become more visible, the facilitator can take these into account in creating a context favourable to change.

The experience gained by the group through use of these techniques enables people to view a situation differently, to endow it with fresh meaning, or to be surprised by a new piece of information. When people come to *perceive* their situation differently in this way, they also come to *understand* it differently, and this is a process that frequently gives rise to original solutions, in the wake of which changes can be observed in the ways in which persons relate to one another.

Summary Part 3

Five techniques are described in detail:

- Doubling is a technique that enables one person, standing close to another, to say something 'on behalf of' this second person, after which the second person takes over to state where s/he stands in relation to what has been said, with the opportunity to expand, correct or modify.

- The Empty Chair technique supplies an additional dimension to the exchange by bringing in an absent person, group or entity whose presence is represented by an empty chair.

- The Empathy Circle enables one member of the group, with the support of all the others, to play the role of a significant person who is not present.

- The Revealing Chairs allow incorporation of the context and encourage the group to see the situation from different angles.

- The Analogical Detours facilitate new ways of seeing, making use of participants' symbolic and creative faculties but without any role-playing. Four forms of this technique are illustrated here: Metaphors, Shapes and Colours, Symbolic Objects and Similar-Sounding Words.

Thirty-three reference sheets for group facilitation

Great teachers create space for learning and invite people into that space.

– Peter Senge

Reference sheet 1: absences and late arrivals

A late arrival can be of help to the group

Aim

To enable each participant to feel fully involved in the process, and help the group to learn to use as a lever anything that happens in the here and now.

Reference in the book

Part 2 refers to the importance of involvement in the here and now.

How

Leaving an empty chair

Leave one or more empty chairs in the circle to represent persons who are absent, late, or who have had to leave the group early.

Working on connections

When a person who has been absent returns to the group, or if someone arrives late, take a few moments to consider the connections between this person and the rest of the group.

Putting it into words

To the group:

- *Could I ask you to give your colleague who has just arrived one sentence or image that sums up the work we have been doing?*

To the person who returns after an absence or who has arrived late:

- *After listening to what your colleagues had to say, could you perhaps now say something about how it links up with what you were doing or how you were feeling before you arrived?*

Reference sheet 2: action techniques

Every choice leads to effects and every effect has meaning

Aim

To select the action technique that seems most pertinent at a given moment in the group process.

Reference in the book

Part 3, instructions for the use of action techniques.

How

Each facilitator can use his/her own techniques and create variations. Each of the techniques mentioned here is described in detail in one of the reference sheets. By way of illustration, we here supply a few non-exhaustive indications for use of the techniques:

Exploring one individual's inner dynamic

- Empathy Circle (in the absence of the person concerned)
- Doubling

Representing the context

- Revealing Chairs (possibly with the use of coloured sheets of paper or objects)
- Analogical Detours, including use of symbolic objects to represent a situation

Enabling the group as a whole to participate

- Empathy Circle
- Analogical Detours: Metaphors, Shapes and Colours, Symbolic Objects, Similar-sounding Words. Using the Analogical Detours, participants can easily work in sub-groups.
- Doubling
- Empty Chair
- Revealing Chairs

Mobilising physically just a few willing members of the group

- Doubling
- Empty Chair
- Revealing Chairs
- Analogical Detours: i.e. suggest that two participants produce a creative representation for the rest of the group

Individual work

- Analogical Detours: Metaphors, Shapes and Colours, Symbolic Objects
- Work with Picture Cards
- Doubling
- Empty Chair

Role-playing without too much movement

- Empathy Circle

Encouraging creativity rather than role-playing

- Analogical Detours

Facilitating groups of one hundred persons or more (Reference sheet 18)

- Analogical Detours: with time for creation in sub-groups as well as some time in the group as a whole.

Putting it into words

Facilitator's inner monologue:

- *Am I going to opt for an action method involving the group as a whole or for an individual approach? How am I going to vary the approach so that participants continue to experience surprise? Is this the right moment to choose a technique that involves dividing participants up into sub-groups? In the context of this particular group, which technique is likely to prove most suitable?*

Reference sheet 3: Analogical Detours

Detours can sometimes speed up progress

Aim

To stimulate participants to enter a symbolic mindset, activate their creativity by exploring the dynamic of a creative representation.

Reference in the book

Part 3, technique 5.

How

Through the use of creativity based on recourse to analogies

- Metaphors (Reference sheet 19),
- Shapes and Colours (Reference sheet 26),
- Symbolic Objects (Reference sheet 30),
- Similar-sounding Words (Reference sheet 28),
- Or any other technique that facilitates, through symbolic means, achievement of another level of reading of a context or question.

Possibility of introducing detours in 'spontaneous' or 'sequential' version

- Spontaneous version: bring in detours gradually and unobtrusively.
- Sequential version: organise an exercise, with a beginning and an end.

Suggest finding a title for the collective representation

- Emphasise the existence and identity of what has been created.

Interact with the creation, stimulate sharing and the search for action paths

- Simultaneously, prompt participants (Reference sheet 16), share (Reference sheet 27), and seek connections with the initial question and paths and action strategies (Reference sheet 32).
  - Towards what is the gaze drawn?
  - What associations can be made?
  - What strikes you in particular?

- In what way does the creative representation provide information of relevance to the initial question?
- What could be the paths and action strategies that emerge from this work?

Putting it into words

Facilitator's interior monologue:

- *On the basis of what I can observe in this group, what is my hypothesis and what type of creative detour am I going to allow myself to propose?*

Reference sheet 4: the ARC

One step after another

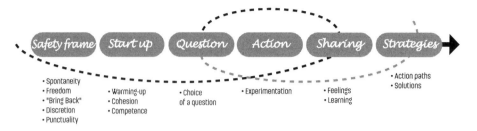

- Spontaneity
- Freedom
- "Bring Back"
- Discretion
- Punctuality

- Warming-up
- Cohesion
- Competence

- Choice of a question

- Experimentation

- Feelings
- Learning

- Action paths
- Solutions

Aim

To allow a means of working with the action methods that is set within an overall procedure constituted by a sequence of stages – 'before', 'during', and 'after'. This process is secured by a frame, a sequence, and by methodological and theoretical reference points.

Reference in the book

Part 3, instructions for use of action techniques.

How

The content and significance of the various stages will vary depending on the context, purpose of the exercise and the technique being used. However, Stage 1 – the safety frame – will be indispensable in any work using action methods.

1: Safety frame stage: Reference sheet 25

2: Start-up stage: Reference sheet 31

3: Question stage: Reference sheet 21

4: Action stage: Reference sheet 2

5: Sharing stage: Reference sheet 27

6: Strategies stage: Reference sheet 32

Putting it into words

'Our work will take place in several stages. Rather than seeking an immediate answer to the question with which we are dealing, we will prefer the option of taking a detour via an 'action experience', an experiment conducted in the here and now. In this way we will create information that will enable us to advance towards our goal'.

Reference sheet 5: client's needs

Meeting the client and his/her context

Aim

To enable the client, the person requesting the facilitator's services, to gain an initial sense of what the use of action techniques entails.

Reference in the book

This reference sheet brings together various points dealt with in the three first parts of the book.

How

Start out from an assumption of the client's competence

- Seek to become sensitive to his genius or skills.

Co-construct the project with the client

- Adapt it as much as possible to the organisational context.
- If possible, include some action techniques from the outset so as to bring the situation to life. It is a question of enabling the client to gain a sense of the methodological specificity of the action techniques. For example:
    - Use of chairs or other objects to represent the context described by the client.
    - Use of Shapes and Colours and other graphical representations to illustrate the situation described.
    - Use of an empty chair to represent the organisation or the company.

Putting it into words

'Could you say a few words about what has prompted you to consult us? How would you formulate the problem with which you have to deal? In order to gain a better understanding of your situation, would you allow me to use the cups here on the table to represent the context you are describing and to enable me to check out with you whether I have properly understood?'

Reference sheet 6: cohesion

In union lies strength

Aim

To activate connections among participants and help the group to develop an identity and autonomy.

Reference in the book

Part 2, Key 3.

How

The work on what connects people may be set in motion using the Spectrogram technique.

Ask participants to position themselves in relation to an imaginary line

- Define an imaginary line running between two parts of the room.
- One end of the line represents 'the most' (e.g. most years of service) and the other end 'the least' (e.g. least years of service).
- Ask people to come to stand along this line on the basis of a chosen criterion: number of kilometres travelled, or number of years of service, or prior knowledge of the subject being dealt with at the training session, etc.

Prompt people to speak

- Ask those who wish to speak to tell the group as a whole why they positioned themselves as they did.

Ask participants to gather in sub-groups

- There exists the possibility of asking people to form groups with their neighbours along this imaginary line.
- Ask people to talk together about factors that connect them:
    - Either in a broad sense: 'What are the connecting links among you?'
    - Or by focussing on the topic, project or purpose of the meeting: 'What are the connecting factors among you in relation to the topic of our gathering?'

Encourage the creation of a message for the group as a whole

- It may be proposed that each sub-group create a message that it wishes to offer to the group as a whole.
- Ask each sub-group to express its message to the group as a whole.

Putting it into words

'I would ask you to stand up now and move around in the space available and then come to position yourselves, on this imaginary diagonal line running between the two corners of the room, in relation to the number of years that you have been working in this company. Those with the longest years of service should place themselves near the window and those only recently recruited at the other end of this diagonal line.

Now that you have found your places, I would propose that you form a group with your neighbours to the left and right of you on the line and that you talk about some factors that connect you. Then I will invite you to create a message that will be addressed by your specific sub-group to the rest of the group'.

Reference sheet 7: competences

The leavening agent of all construction

Aim

To increase a group's capacity for action, autonomy and emancipation.

Reference in the book

Part 2, Key 4.

How

Encourage people to express their talents

- Begin a working session with a question that invites participants and the group to express where their skills lie.

Develop a way of seeing that is geared to competence

- Lend support to the resources of persons and groups even when they themselves claim that they lack resources or express doubts on this score, e.g. 'If I were to put it differently, I would say that your sense of failure also indicates an ability to call yourself into question'.
- Become accustomed to observing, and naming, 'professional genius' (Part 1, Inner Attitude 4).

Recognise the place of each person

- Pay attention to ensuring that each person is made to feel present:
- Leave an empty chair to represent a person who is a temporarily absent member of the group.
- Grant the requisite time and space to welcome a person who joins the group part way through the proceedings.

Putting it into words

'What you have just shared is an indication of your personal competence. Thanks to your sense of observation and your inner work, you found a new way of moving forward'.

Reference sheet 8: completing the group experience

Saying goodbye in the group

Aim

To enable the group to put a satisfying end to its work and to say goodbye.

Reference in the book

The importance of this completion process is referred to in Part 2.

How

Each facilitator can create a personal ritual that accords with his/her own style as well as with the context. Examples are offered below.

Ritual standing in a circle

- Suggest that participants stand up and come to form a circle around an empty sheet of paper placed on the floor. Each participant, before leaving, will symbolically set down on this sheet something that they wish to 'leave behind': for example, an impression of the day's work, a feeling, an image, etc.

Ritual using cards or objects

- Participants are asked to place on a large sheet spread out on the floor an object or picture card that represents for them the work that the group has carried out together during the session.

- Each participant shows to the group his/her chosen item and says a few words about it.

- Participants then pick up an object that is not their own and return it to the person who put it down earlier, saying something that they feel they would like to tell the person in question.

Putting it into words

'Now I would ask you all to stand up and together choose a coloured sheet of paper that will represent the work we have done here together. We will place the sheet of paper on the floor and form a circle around it. This will be something like a tablecloth on which we can symbolically place whatever it is that we would like to set down and leave behind us when we go. What is it that you would like to say before leaving? Is there something you would like to tell one or several other participants? Now is no longer the moment for back-and-forward dialogue and response. Simply put something down. And then we will take three deep breaths all together, leave this group behind us, and go our separate ways. As we sometimes say: 'the circle opens up but the work goes on".

Reference sheet 9: de-roling or exiting the role

Role-playing can be an intense experience so we mustn't forget to leave the role behind us

Aim

To enable persons who have played a role to regain full contact with themselves.

Reference in the book

Part 3, instructions for use of action techniques.

How

Use movement and voice

● Say out loud: 'I have role-played . . . (state the name of the person whose role one has played) and now I am . . . (say one's own name)'.

● Slide the hands along one's own body as if divesting oneself of a garment.

● Stamp one's feet several times, or make other physical efforts intended to restore groundedness.

● Where the experience has been emotionally overpowering, jump up and down three times and say 'I am . . . (give one's own first name)'.

Putting away the equipment

● Use the moment of putting away the equipment as an opportunity for closure, saying one last word about the experience undergone.

Putting it into words

'And now, in order to conclude, I would ask each of you to help put away the objects we have been using (sheets of paper, empty chair, etc.). And while you are putting whatever it is away, you can also state out loud in what way this item or these objects have contributed to your experience'.

Reference sheet 10: Doubling

Empathy in action

Aim

To animate and lend validity to inner experience so that individual participants and groups come more closely into contact with emotions, visions and strategies.

Reference in the book

Part 3, technique 1.

How

Request agreement

- Ask a person whether s/he agrees to be doubled (with an explanation of what this means).

Come physically closer together

- If the person agrees, stand close to her, at just a slight angle and further back.
- If the person agrees, one hand may be placed on her shoulder.

Speak on behalf of the person

- Without looking at her, begin to speak on behalf of the other person using the 'I' form (1st person singular). 'I, (state the person's name), think that . . . feel that . . . well, this is how I see things . . .'

Ask the person 'whether one might say that . . .'

- Allow the person being doubled to supply additional detail, correct, expand.

Proposing Doubling in 'spontaneous' mode

- Explain the Doubling technique to the group.
- Explain that, if one person in the group would like to double another, other than in an exercise specifically geared to doubling, he or she should first ask the facilitator whether s/he agrees that a doubling should take place at this particular point.
- Decide whether the doubling can take place at this precise point in the work.

- If it is decided that doubling may take place at this point, remind the person proposing to double of the need to request agreement from the person s/he proposes to double.

Proposing Doubling in 'sequential' mode

- Identify a situation or question

- Suggest that a person concerned by the question should move his/her chair forward.

- Suggest that participants who so wish should come to double the 'bearer' of the question, proposing ideas, hypotheses, goals, strategies, connected with the initial question.

- In relation to each comment or proposal, ask the person being doubled to say whether or not they are willing to 'take it on board'.

- Explain to the person being doubled that she is also quite free to take on board only a part of what is being said in the process of doubling.

Putting it into words

- Mary, would you agree to let us say something on your behalf about the strategies to be developed in your team context?
- Now I invite any group members who so wish to stand up and come forward to double Mary, first checking that she agrees to this. You may, if Mary agrees, place your hand on her shoulder. As you are speaking on Mary's behalf, you should use the first person singular 'I' form.
- Mary, after each doubling contribution you will be invited to say whether or not you feel able to take it on board on the basis of your own feelings and convictions.

Reference sheet 11: Empathy Circle

All are concentrated around one role

Aim

To enable the group better to get to know a significant person who is not present.

Reference in the book

Part 3, technique 3.

How

Start out from a situation in which a problematic relationship exists between two persons because, for example, of unresolved tensions or ill-defined responsibilities. The person whose role is being played is not present.

Place an empty chair close to the facilitator

- Ask the person most closely concerned by the question whether s/he agrees to role-play the person chosen.
- Place an empty chair close to oneself for this participant.

Ask the group to frame questions in the first person singular ('I' form).

- Begin oneself by asking some simple factual questions. Example: 'How old am I?'
- Then, encourage group members to take over, making sure that they too use the first person singular.
- Make sure that the person playing the role does not speak on her/his own behalf but from the standpoint of the person whose role s/he is playing.

Exiting the role (de-roling):

- Step 1: Exchange one's own seat with that of the person who has played the role. Ask the role-player to say how or what s/he felt while playing that role: 'What was your experience while playing that role?'
- Step 2: Help the role-player to come out of the role. Stand up with him/her, ask him/her to say his/her own name in a loud voice, to stamp his/her feet, to shake arms and hands, vigorously rub his/her clothes.

- Step 3: Invite the person to say something about the effects experienced as a result of playing the role. Invite him/her to return to his/her initial seat and then ask, 'What was it like for you to play this role?'

Sharing and the search for action paths and strategies

- Continue with the group sharing process (Reference sheet 27).

- Question to the group: 'what struck you most about what has just taken place?'

- Accompany the search for action strategies in relation to the initial question (Reference sheet 32).

Putting it into words

'We will now take some time to make the person about whom we are speaking more present. It is important to realise that when someone has played the role of another and then sees that person again, it will no longer be quite the same; some micro-changes will be observable'.

Reference sheet 12: Empty Chair

Stepping back to let in some surprise effects

Aim

To enable several persons to give voice to a third party who may be a person, a group, the company, a project, a product, a competitor, the founder, the client, the claimant, etc.

Reference in the book

Part 3, technique 2.

How

If use is made of the Empty Chair technique at a team meeting or in some other group context without an external facilitator, then a member of the group takes on the role of 'action facilitator'.

Introducing an empty chair

- If there is a table, place an additional chair around the table.
- The empty chair may be used to facilitate or back up an exchange, even if there is no explicit initial question.

Suggest that participants should give voice to the chair

- 'Anyone who so wishes may stand up, go to stand behind a chair, and say something by giving voice to this chair. You speak on behalf of the chair, in the 1st person singular, as 'I''.

Spontaneous version

Bring in a chair that can be 'personified' as and when appropriate, throughout the group work. At any point in the proceedings, any participant who so wishes may stand up and say something on behalf of the empty chair. A sharing time follows the intervention and then, where appropriate, a time for seeking paths and action strategies.

Sequential version

Here it is a case of deliberately inserting into the proceedings an 'exercise period' using the empty chair.

- 'Now we will take 15 minutes to conduct an experiment . . . .'

Sharing and the search for paths and action strategies

- Depending on the context, a sharing period may be introduced (Reference sheet 27).
- If a question has been identified, time should be allowed to seek strategies (Reference sheet 32).

Putting it into words

'Might it not be a good idea to pause here for a few moments to represent what the founder of the organisation experienced during his mandate? If you agree, I would propose that we bring in an empty chair to represent the founder. I wonder whether each of you would agree to come forward to say something on his behalf. This might help us to see more clearly where we are up to today and what challenges we face'.

Reference sheet 13: ethical considerations

Spontaneity is vulnerable and needs our protection

Aim

To enable the group to feel sufficiently safe.

Reference in the book

Part 3, instructions for the use of action techniques.

How

Communication

In line with the rule on discretion (Reference sheet 25), ask yourself whether participants have received sufficient prior information concerning the boundaries between what may and what may not be passed on to third parties (hierarchy, team, commissioner, competitor, family, etc.).

Full consideration for persons present

Bear in mind that it is the feelings, knowledge, representations and words spoken by participants that are to be regarded as the starting and finishing point of the work.

Professional experience and attitude

Ask yourself whether, as a facilitator, you are sufficiently well-prepared and whether you possess the requisite skills and experience to practise action techniques:

- Have I carried out the necessary work on my inner attitudes in the context of a sustained personal development endeavour?
- Have I internalised the keys for accompanying a group process?
- Have I experimented for and on myself the action techniques and gained an understanding of their mechanisms and benefits?

Putting it into words

Facilitator's interior monologue:

– *Do I have sufficient openness and inner depth and transparency to receive and take in whatever emerges, or do I need to take care of myself and pay attention to my own lived experience as facilitator? Have I supplied the group with all necessary information about the context and boundaries of the work, the rule of discretion, the kind of information that may and that may not be passed on to persons outside the group? Am I well enough prepared to use this technique? Do I have sufficient personal experience of its use?*

Reference sheet 14: function of the unspoken

Making sense of experience

Aim

To enable the group to move forward in a spirit and posture of (re)search and to build constantly on new findings.

Reference in the book

Part 2, Key 5.

How

From a general stance

- Read everything that is going on or that 'takes place' in a group as signalling important information circulating within the system.
- Start out from the assumption that *whatever* is happening is in the service of balance within the group.

This general stance becomes all the more relevant where the situation is in some way uncomfortable or unexpected

- Seek to supply positive connotations in relation to whatever may have been disruptive or have generated discomfort.
- Consider the interplay among all aspects and features of what happens.
- Ask questions that seek connections between several pieces of information even if one does not oneself have an answer.
- Place one's trust also in the group's own power of co-construction.

Putting it into words

'What might be the 'function' of what is taking place *here* at this very moment? What could it be telling us? How does what is happening *now* serve the group interest? What links can we find between what is happening here now and the subject on which we have come together to work? What analogies might suggest themselves?'

Reference sheet 15: inner attitude cards

Inner attitude is the guide to every intervention

Aim

To enable the group to gain a sense of ways of working on the self.

Reference in the book

Part 1.

How

Create a set of attitude cards

Prepare a set of cards by writing a summary of significant inner attitudes on separate sheets of coloured paper or cardboard.

Ask the group to draw a card from the pack

Before closing the session, as a means of helping the group to internalise some of the attitudes stimulated during the work, ask participants to draw a card from the pack and say something about the inner attitude mentioned on it.

Putting it into words

'Here is a set of cards. I will hold them face downwards and ask you to draw any card from the pack. I would ask you to turn the card over, read it, and then see what connections you can make between that card, the work we have been doing here today, and your own professional practice'.

Reference sheet 16: interacting with a creation

Be daring

Aim

To enable the group to derive maximum benefit from its creation by taking its insights further.

Reference in the book

Part 3, instructions for use of action techniques.

How

Stimulating creative thinking

- Draw attention to details, analogies, a feeling for colour, spatial configuration, and all kinds of fantasies that might be unleashed by this representation.
- Make connections, take note of complex, paradoxical or disconcerting aspects or components.

Welcoming surprise effects

- Focus attention on whatever prompts surprise. Question the surprise, make it more explicit, take steps to extend or deepen it.

Putting it into words

- Do you see or hear something that prompts surprise?
- What can you associate with what you are seeing?
- What kind of fantasies come into your mind?
- Which particular details attract your attention?
- What do you find particularly striking?
- What can we say about this choice of image?

– What can we say about the colours that have been used for this picture?

– What can we say about how space has been used to write on this sheet of paper, and about the way the available space has been structured?

– What is important about what has just happened?

Reference sheet 17: keys to activate collective intelligence

Diving deep into the meeting with the group

Aim

To foster collective intelligence.

Reference in the book

Part 2.

How

Key 1: Working with the here and now

What am I going to put in place so as to remain attentive to all that is happening in the here and now and use it to move towards my goal?

Key 2: Creating a safety frame

How am I going to create the conditions required for participants to experience trust? What will be the important points to be made explicit from the outset?

Key 3: Stimulating cohesion

In what ways will I enable participants to develop a sense of connection with each other?

Key 4: Strengthening skills

What are the skills that I know or sense are present and how will I make use of them in this instance? How will I stimulate 'give and take' within the group?

Key 5: Taking account of what is unspoken

On what elements of my observation will I be able to develop hypotheses? What is there that remains unspoken and yet seemingly functional within the system?

Key 6: Viewing a same situation from a different angle

What detours will I choose to activate participants' representations and set them in movement? How can I create surprise effects?

Key 7: Remain on a searching path

What do I observe? What is my hypothesis? To what form of intervention will I choose to give priority?

Putting it into words

Facilitator's internal monologue:

> – *I arrive tired and weighed down by personal concerns, but before starting out on the work I make myself available to meet the group on its own ground in the here and now. I breathe. I compose myself into a state of availability, a posture of searching and ready for co-construction. So here we go!*

Reference sheet 18: large group

Mobilising the organisation as a whole

Aim

To enable a large group to move forward together in the direction of change.

Reference in the book

Part 2, Key 3, and also the principles governing the action techniques described in Part 3.

How

Working with the Analogical Detours, through the preparation of creative representations, is one means of mobilising groups of as many as a hundred persons. In such cases, microphones and a projector will be required.

Identifying the initial question

● Reformulate, together with the group, the initial question.

Invite participants to prepare creative representations in sub-groups

● Ask participants to form randomised sub-groups and to prepare a creation that is in some way connected with the initial question.

● Supply the equipment required to enable each sub-group to produce a creative representation. This 'equipment' may consist of drawing materials and/or symbolic objects (Reference sheets 26 & 30).

● Ask participants to find names for their creation and to come to write all titles on a large panel that is visible to all.

● Take photos of the creative representations and project them to the group as a whole.

● Ask a representative of each sub-group to come to present the creation and its title to the assembly.

Prompt participants and stimulate sharing and the search for action paths

● Interact with the creation (Reference sheet 16), and share (Reference sheet 27), seeking connections with the initial question as well as strategies (Reference sheet 32).

The following questions may be dealt with in sub-groups (with subsequent reporting back to the group as a whole) or directly in the assembly by allowing a limited number of persons to speak.

- *What turned out to be most striking about the various creative representations projected?*
- *What associations suggest themselves?*
- *What can each one of us learn?*
- *How do the creative representations supply information about the initial question?*
- *What paths and action strategies emerge from this work?*

● Suggest that participants take note of proposals so that they can be collected together for the purpose of using collective intelligence to move in the direction of the stated goal.

Putting it into words

'Now I am going to ask you to divide up and form groups of seven, making sure that these sub-groups are well mixed. In relation to the question that we have come here to discuss today, namely, the obstacles currently limiting cooperation among your different services and the potential resources offered by improved cooperation, I would like you to produce a creative representation using the objects placed at your disposal. Then, during a second stage, you will give your creation a title on which you will have the opportunity to comment during the projection'.

Reference sheet 19: Metaphor

Logic will take you from A to B; imagination will take you everywhere—*Albert Einstein*

Aim

To enable the group to make use of the creative dynamic unleashed by a metaphor.

Reference in the book

Part 3, one form of technique 5.

How

Ask participants to illustrate a situation by one or several metaphors

- Any form of illustrative analogy may be used, rooted in colours, sensations, proverbs, scenarios, including a link with a film, song or painting.
- Participants are asked to give a name to the metaphor.

Prompt the group to seek sharing and the search for action paths

- At the same time interact with the metaphor (Reference sheet 16) in ways that will enable participants to enter into it, explore it, decode it, seek out its dynamic. Encourage participants to share what the metaphor evokes for each of them (Reference sheet 27). Help participants to make connections between the different stages and facets of the metaphor and the initial situation they set out to explore. In this way, gradually lead the group towards the search for strategies (Reference sheet 32).

Putting it into words

- Now that a situation has been presented, what metaphor would you associate with it? (Allow metaphors to emerge). Now that you have heard all the metaphors, which one are you going to select as being the most alive for you in relation to the situation we have described? (Allow the group or the person to choose one metaphor.)

- Now let us focus on this metaphor. How could we together describe its dynamic force? What connections can we find between what we have said and the situation on which we are working? What else comes to mind on the basis of this analogy? How does it throw light on the situation from which we started out?

Reference sheet 20: picture cards

A picture is worth ten thousand words

Aim

To activate creative thinking with the help of images.

Reference in the book

Part 3, technique 5, this is an additional form of Analogical Detours not described in the book.

How

Choose a set of picture cards

- Cards on which there is no writing enable people to project themselves broadly.
- It is quite possible to create a photo-language of one's own.

Ask participants to draw three cards

- Present the cards face down.
- If the question being dealt with concerns one person in particular, ask that person not to draw any cards.

Ask participants to select one of the three cards drawn

- Ask them to choose the one that best represents the situation under discussion or the question initially raised.
- Collect back together the cards that have not been chosen.

Invite each participant to lay down the chosen card

- Ask participants to lay the cards on a large sheet visible to all.
- If possible, place the sheet on the floor in the centre.

Ask questions or make comments to stimulate sharing and the search for action paths

- When one participant is more particularly concerned by the initial question:
    - Ask that person to speak first.
    - Encourage him/her to react to the representation offered by the group (Reference sheet 16).

 – Ask him/her to say something about any connections perceived with the situation s/he initially presented.

● Encourage the group to interact with the cards (Reference sheet 16) and to explore the dynamic of the creative representation. Ask participants to share these responses (Reference sheet 27) and to say what prompted them to choose the card they did. Accompany the search for action paths and strategies.

Putting it into words

'I will come to each of you with a set of picture cards and ask you to draw three from the pack. When each of you has drawn three cards, you will look at them and choose whichever one of your own three cards seems most relevant to the situation on which we are working. You will return the other cards to me and will then be able to place your chosen card on the floor, on the large sheet of paper'.

Reference sheet 21: question stage

Learning to trim the sails

Aim

To enable the group to clarify and formulate what it is seeking to understand and to achieve.

Reference in the book

Part 3, instructions for use of action techniques.

How

Helping the group to formulate its question

- Suggest that participants share, in sub-groups, the questions that arise for them.
- Ask each sub-group to select one question and then bring it into the group as a whole.

Possibility of organising a 'sociometric choice'

The 'sociometric choice' places the selection of the question to be dealt with in the hands of the group.

- Ask the participants who contributed a question to the group to stand up and position themselves somewhere within the working area.
- Then ask the other members of the group to come to stand behind the person representing the question that they would wish to select, possibly placing a hand on this person's shoulder.
- An alternative approach is to represent each question not by a person but by a sheet of paper or object, for example a scarf placed on the floor. This enables every participant to have a say, including those who have contributed the questions, by standing behind one of the items placed on the floor.
- This spatial representation creates an 'image' of the group position at this point in time and can help to make it clear which of the questions posed is the one to be tackled by the group in the ensuing session.

Take up once again with the group a question that has been formulated at an earlier stage

- If the question to be dealt with has already been formulated outside the group, then it can be reformulated and reviewed in the group. This enables work to take place on how the group identifies with the question and believes in it its significance.
- If necessary, make some adjustments to the initial question.

Putting it into words

'I would ask you all to stand up now and to move close to the person representing the question that you consider most important for us to tackle in this group session. You don't need to think in terms of 'the best question' but rather to consider which of the proposed questions feels most relevant to you here today on the basis of your experience and current situation'.

Reference sheet 22: (re)search posture

The path taken is just as important as the destination

Purpose

To enable the group to feel accompanied in its movement.

Reference in the book

Part 2, Key 7.

How

Observe

- Observe what is said, whether verbally or non-verbally; and also what is not said either verbally or non-verbally.
- Observe the interplay among participants.
- Observe what is going on in one's own individual mind and body.

Create one or more hypotheses

- What do I understand from what is going on?
- What do I associate with what is going on?
- How do I interpret what is going on?
- How does any of this link up with my own specific approach and reference materials?
- What is my hypothesis?

Choose a mode of intervention

- Will I choose to communicate to the group what I have observed?
- Will I choose to accompany the group's own movement or rather seek to give it a direction?
- Will I place more emphasis on work with the group as a whole or on work conducted in sub-groups?
- Will I choose to use an action method? If so, which one?
- Am I going to say something, or choose to remain silent for a while?

Another stage of observation

- How is the group reacting to what has just happened?

- Am I able to observe that certain specific pieces of information have become more explicit?

Then return to observing the overall situation. Create one or more hypotheses. Choose a mode of intervention. Observe once again. In this way continue and build up a continuing research cycle.

Putting it into words

Facilitator's internal monologue:

> – *I observe that there is one person in this group who says nothing and another who hardly stops speaking. I would hypothesise that this has something to do with the balance of power. And at this precise moment we are deciding how to distribute the roles for the tasks that we will be performing. The way we deal with the balance of power in our midst is going to be fundamental for carrying out this project. I'm going to suggest that we take a few moments to speak about how we see each participant's position in the project. As we have already done a lot of talking, I'll propose a Shapes and Colours exercise.*

Reference sheet 23: resuming a session after a break

Coming back together again

Aim

To co-construct a thread to connect the different meetings.

Reference in the book

The importance of this process is referred to in Part 2.

How

Propose that participants say in turn 'My name is . . . and what I remember is . . .'.

● Suggest that each participant speak in turn, reminding the group of his/her first name and then referring to a memory of something that happened or was said during the earlier or preceding session.

Propose the creation of a metaphor

● Invite participants, individually or in sub-groups, to create a metaphor that is representative of what they experienced during the preceding work session.

● Participants may also produce a creative representation using shapes and colours or select an object to represent the preceding session.

Putting it into words

'I would propose that we resume our work by telling one another 'what we brought to this session' and 'what we have left behind''.

Reference sheet 24: Revealing Chairs

Expanding our vision

Aim

To bring a group to locate and view a situation in its context.

Reference in the book

Part 3, technique 4.

How

Reflect with participants upon persons, groups, organisations, concepts or entities that are of significance in the context.

Placing the chairs

- Ask the group, or the person most closely concerned by the initial question, to position the chairs representing significant persons, groups, organisations, concepts or entities in the context.
- One person gets up at a time.
- Stand up and move around, accompanying participants in their efforts to position the chairs appropriately, paying attention to their direction, superposing them or placing them at a distance from one another, etc.

Analyse the arrangement

- Ask people to say 'what strikes them' and what observations they can make about the way the chairs have been positioned in relation to one another. Is there anything that surprises them? Is there some reaction they would like to share?

Give voice to the chairs

- Standing, invite participants who so wish to take on roles and give voice to the chairs.
- Allow participants who so wish to go to stand behind any chair of their choice with the exception of one that represents them personally, if such is the case (it is acceptable, however, for a participant to speak from behind a chair representing a group or entity to which s/he belongs).

- If, for any reason, people have difficulty in coming forward, the facilitator can repeat, standing behind the chairs, whatever it is that participants are saying from their places.
- It is possible to replace chairs by 'post-its', objects, coloured or plain sheets of paper, etc.

Optional component: moving the chairs around

- Suggest to participants that they alter the position of some chairs: 'If you were to make some changes to the way the chairs are arranged in relation to each other, what would these changes be? Just say what you feel about how they have been positioned'.
- Make sure that just one person at a time comes forward to try out a change in the arrangement of the chairs.
- Ask participants to say something about what the repositioning means to them, and how others respond to the change.

Sharing and the search for paths and action strategies

- Give the floor to participants who have played roles and to the rest of the group to enable them to say what they felt, observed, found to be of particular importance (Reference sheet 27).
- Accompany the search for strategies (Reference sheet 32).

Putting it into words

'We are going to represent the situation we are speaking about together with its context. I would like you to identify aspects that seem worth representing, whether these be persons either present or absent, ideas, groups, organisations, concepts, or any other factor or entity that is, has been, or will be, important in the context of which we are speaking'.

Reference sheet 25: safety frame

The safety frame is the group's skin

Aim

To help build up trust in the group.

Reference in the book

Part 2, Key 2.

How

State the rules at the beginning and offer reminders if and when necessary

- Spontaneity: participants within the group should feel free to give expression to feelings or to whatever comes into their minds.
- Freedom: each participant is free to accept or to decline any component of the proposed experiment but is expected to remain within the work area during the time allocated for group sessions.
- 'Bring back': anything that is of relevance to the group may be brought back into the group.
- Discretion: more personal elements disclosed within the group are not to be revealed beyond its confines.
- Punctuality: each working period has a beginning and an end. Agreed work schedules are to be clearly stated and observed.

Proposing an 'action ritual': the confidentiality circle

This practice may be performed at the beginning and/or end of the session:

- Ask participants to stand up, form a circle, and to direct their right hand, palm down, towards the centre of the circle.
- Ask everyone to close the four fingers of this hand, leaving the thumb facing naturally outwards at a right angle.
- Suggest that each participant enclose their neighbour's thumb in their own closed four fingers.

In this way a second circle of hands linked by thumbs is formed within the circle of persons. An idea may then be suggested whereby each participant can signify his/her agreement to abide by the rule of discretion. For example:

- Suggest that each person, in turn, should pronounce his or her own first name with the intention of directing it into the centre of the confidentiality circle.
- Suggest that each person send a sound, or name a colour, to be sent symbolically into the confidentiality circle.
- Ask participants to make silent inner contact with their undertaking in relation to discretion.

When all participants have spoken their first names, the hands let go of each other.

Putting it into words

'Before beginning our work, we will agree on a set of rules as follows (enumerate the five rules). Do you agree to continue on this basis? Do you have any questions? Would you like to add any other rules for your own comfort and that of the group?'

Reference sheet 26: Shapes and Colours

Make way for the creative instinct to express itself

Aim

Together to clarify and throw light on the essential dynamic of a situation by means of a graphical and symbolic representation.

Reference in the book

Part 3, one form of technique 5.

How

It is preferable to use the term 'creative representation' (rather than 'drawing') and to explain that one does not need 'to know how to draw' in order to derive benefit from this experimental task.

Propose that participants work in sub-groups

- Divide group members into sub-groups. Ask each sub-group to create, on a large sheet, a presentation that has some connection with the initial question being asked or explored.

- When the presentations are finished, ask each sub-group to find a title for its presentation and to write this title on the same sheet.

- Then ask the sub-groups to bring their presentations together and place them in a central position on the floor from where they can be seen by all.

- Ask participants to stand up and walk around the presentations so as to become familiar with them. This part of the experiment takes place in silence.

- Invite participants to return to their seats and ask them what they noticed or were particularly struck by during their discovery of the various creations.

This experimental technique can be used in large groups of more than 100 persons (Reference sheet 18).

Propose an arrangement whereby two participants present a creation on behalf of the group

● Ask two members of the group to represent on large sheets, using shapes and colours, some aspect or element of what they perceive in the discourse employed by the rest of the group. Arrange for these two participants to work with their backs to the others and ensure that the rest of the group cannot see what they are producing.

● After about a quarter of an hour halt the exchange that is underway and ask the two group members who have been working on 'representations' to bring their creations forward and place them on the floor where everyone can see them.

Prompt and stimulate sharing and the search for action paths

● Interact with the creative representation (Reference sheet 16) and encourage sharing (Reference sheet 27) by seeking links with the initial question and possible action strategies (Reference sheet 32).

   – What attracts our attention?

   – What associations suggest themselves?

   – In what ways do you feel personally implicated or inspired by this creative representation?

   – (to the persons who produced the representation) On hearing what your colleagues have to say about their perceptions of your creative representation, do you gain a sense that they have understood you?

   – What kind of information is supplied by the collective representation in relation to the initial question?

   – What paths and action strategies might be suggested by this work?

Putting it into words

'Now you will view and familiarise yourselves with the panels your colleagues have produced and this will give you the opportunity to consider what features they may share and in what respects they differ from one another (allow 5 minutes). Now let us return to our seats. What did you find particularly striking? What are the fantasies or associations that come to mind? What would you like to share with the rest of the group?'

Reference sheet 27: sharing stage

Don't put the carriage before the horses

Aim

To enable participants to share what they themselves have learned during the action experiment.

Reference in the book

Part 3, instructions for use of action methods.

How

Open up a space for sharing responses

- Ask the group as a whole what has been experienced during the experimentation using the action method.
- Ask what connections individuals found that they established with their own professional life and experience.
- Ask what each person learned of personal value to her/him.
- It is possible, but not essential, to specify an order of contributions, for example, begin with those persons who played an active role, followed by the observers, or the other way round.

Adjust and reframe the proceedings if necessary

- If participants begin to give one another advice, interpretations, analyses, or to seek solutions too quickly, intervene to redirect the contributions by reminding participants that this is a period intended specifically for sharing what was experienced during the experiment and that each person is requested to speak just of his or her own experience in this respect.

Putting it into words

'For the time being we are simply sharing our individual responses to the experience we have just been involved in together. Stay with what you experienced, with the feelings that passed through you, the images, sensations, thoughts, whatever was important for you, whatever you feel that you have learned. You can link this up with your own experience. Is there something that you would like to share with us?'

Reference sheet 28: Similar-sounding Words

Guided by the sound

Aim

To stimulate the group to symbolise and represent a situation or a question using an experiment based on writing.

Reference in the book

Part 3, one form of technique 5.

How

Ask participants to make an initial word association

- Ask participants to think of one or more words that they associate, in their own minds, with the initial question or context. These initial word associations will not be revealed to others during the experiment.

- When the words of each of the groups are gathered together it is important that there should be a total of at least eight words.

Ask participants to make a second word association based on sound

- Ask participants to associate to the first word another similar-sounding word, i.e. one ending with the same sound.

- Write all these second words on a large sheet of paper.

Ask participants to compose a written text

- Ask participants, in sub-groups, to compose a text representative of the situation on which the group is working, using for this purpose all the similar-sounding words that have been written on the large sheet.

- This text might be regarded as a means of giving metaphorical expression to the situation.

- An alternative possibility, rather than dividing participants into sub-groups, is to let each person compose an individual text.

- The texts composed must contain, at least, all the similar-sounding words but they may, in addition, contain other words too.

- Participants are given approximately ten minutes to compose their texts.

Asking for each text to be read out

- Ask one person from each sub-group to read out the text composed.

- This stage of reading out loud has a theatrical component. To bring out the full impact of each text, participants should be instructed to read slowly, allowing themselves to enter and give life to the text.

Invite a participant or the group to select one text

- Ask the person who is most particularly affected by the initial question, or the group as a whole, to select one text.

- The selected text will be the one that the individual participant or the group feels to be most alive, in other words, closest to expressing feelings associated with the question or situation on which the group is working.

Interact with the text and stimulate sharing in the search for action paths

At the same time, prompt the group to interact with the text (Reference sheet 16), explore it, decode it, and seek out its dynamic. Encourage participants to share their individual responses to the text (Reference sheet 27). Gradually, assist participants in making connections between the different stages and facets identifiable in the text and the initial situation. Lead the group, in this way, gradually and in small steps, towards the search for strategies (Reference sheet 32).

Putting it into words

- You have just heard a description of a situation. What is the first word that comes to mind in relation to what you have heard? Write it down. This word belongs to you alone. You will not be asked to communicate to the others.

- Now that you have all written down your word, write next to it another word that ends with the same sound even if, in terms of meaning, it has nothing to do with the first word.

- Now that one text has been selected from among those written, what are your associations in relation to this particular text? What images does it bring to mind? What do you find particularly striking? What can you learn from the text? What kind of useful information does the text supply in relation to the situation we are here to work on and develop?

Reference sheet 29: surprise effect

It's all grist to the mill

Aim

To help the group to create new information by recourse to creative thinking.

Reference in the book

Part 2, Key 6.

How

Encourage the group to notice and elaborate upon unexpected connections

- Observe what is taking place in terms of spatial positioning, information emitted by the body (one's own as well as participants'), colours, symbols, words taken 'out of context, and non-verbal expression. Grasp elements of the here and now that seem to have nothing to do with the subject 'officially' under consideration.

- Draw the group's attention to this 'other thing', this feature of the situation that seems to have nothing to do with it.

- Question the group or an individual participant about the connection between this unexpected feature of the situation and whatever else is happening in the here and now of the group.

Putting it into words

- What connections can we make between what has just happened and the subject on which we are working?

- How might the thoughtless doodles or indiscriminate scribbles that we made while speaking or listening connect with the topic with which we are dealing?

- Give me any number between 1 and 150. Then let's see whether the corresponding page of this book might bear some connection with the problem we are endeavouring to solve.

Reference sheet 30: Symbolic Objects

Objects contribute volume and colour to representations

Aim

To enable the group to enter and move within a symbolic dimension through the handling and choice of objects.

Reference in the book

Part 3, one form of technique 5.

How

Ask participants to work together to produce creative representations

- Spread out a selection of items that participants, working in sub-groups, can use to produce creations on large sheets of paper. The objects supplied for this purpose will be extremely varied: cards, felt-tipped pens, a wide range of small articles, soft toys, ropes, wool, shells, pebbles, coins, and so forth.

- Follow the same procedure as in Reference sheet 26 'Shapes and Colours' to encourage sub-groups to produce their creative representations.

Using symbolic objects at the beginning or end of a work group

- At the beginning of a group session, suggest that participants select an object that seems relevant to the subject on which the group is to conduct its work. This may be something that they are wearing on their person or carrying in their bag, or a symbolic object selected from a collection of such items placed at their disposal. Ask participants to place the object of their choice on a support where it will be visible to all, for example on a large sheet of paper placed in the centre on the floor.

- At the end of the experiment, ask participants to select an object they find illustrative of how they experienced this part of the session. All participants will be asked to place their object on the support provided for this purpose, for example a large sheet of paper placed in the centre.

Prompt and stimulate sharing and the search for action paths

- Interact with the creative realisation produced from the collection of items placed on the large sheet of paper. Explore this creative representation, seek its dynamic, decode it (Reference sheet 16). Where appropriate, encourage sharing (Reference sheet 27) and the search for strategies (Reference sheet 32).

Putting it into words

'In order to illustrate the question with which we are dealing, I would suggest that you produce a creation using some of the objects placed at your disposal'.

Reference sheet 31: start-up stage

To set the body in movement is to prepare the mind for change

Aim

To foster spontaneity, encourage trust, bring spatial dynamism into the relationship, prepare the body for action, initiate the work that will follow.

Reference in the book

Part 3, Instructions for use of action techniques.

How

- Propose a warming-up exercise
- Foster cohesion (Reference sheet 6)
- Strengthen a sense of personal competence (Reference sheet 7)

Variations for warming up

- Self-massage session.
- Greet one another shoulder to shoulder, hand to hand, foot to foot.
- Presentation of two persons at a time, after which each of them presents the other by means of doubling.

Putting it into words

'Now I'm going to ask you all to walk around the room. You can feel the contact between your feet and the floor. You can feel the breath that is active in your body . . . the air coming in through the nostrils . . . the air coming out of the nostrils. The temperature of the air. Now you are becoming conscious of all the small movements of the body that enable you to walk. And if thoughts come into your mind, you observe them, rather as if you were in front of a cinema screen'.

Reference sheet 32: strategies stage

When change is triggered

Aim

To take advantage of the work carried out using action techniques to find innovative paths and ways of moving forward together.

Reference in the book

Part 3, instructions for use of action techniques.

How

When the initial question is one affecting the group as a whole

Suggest that the group should seek together, in a spirit of collective intelligence, ways of moving forward and action strategies to be adopted.

If one participant is more specifically affected by the initial question

For the purpose of distancing, introduce an additional experiment that places the person concerned in the position of observer. Allow here for the following three stages:

- Ask the person most affected by the question to listen and not intervene for the time being, while assuring him/her that at the end it is s/he who will have the final word.
- On the basis of the initial question, suggest to the rest of the group that they seek paths and action strategies that would accord with their own experience, skills, resources and references.
- Then ask the person specifically concerned, who was in an observer position, to say something about where s/he is now in relation to the question asked earlier in the proceedings.

Putting it into words

To the participant most affected by the initial question: 'you are the person who raised the question on which we have worked using action techniques. For you this was an experiment during which you have listened to what your colleagues have had to say, and it may well be that some of them are experiencing difficulties similar to those you have described. Now it is your turn to speak:

- *What is particularly alive for you now, at this particular moment?*
- *And/or: what is your message to the group?*
- *And/or: what are you going to take away from this session?*
- *And/or: what have you learned here?*

Reference sheet 33: working space arrangement

Moving from one space to another

Aim

To enable the group to internalise awareness of the boundaries between the 'space for talk' and the 'space for experimentation'.

Reference in the book

Part 3, instructions for use of action techniques.

How

Arrangement of the available space

- Obtain information about the habits and culture of the organisation.
- Choose the spatial arrangement that will best encourage interaction and allow practice of action techniques.
- Prefer whenever possible an arrangement that dispenses with a table and in which participants are seated in a semi-circle or U shape.

Allow space for creative work and space for verbal expression and exchange

- Allow an area for creative work. This is where the action methods will be practised. This area may be in the extension of the U if the chairs are arranged in a semi-circle.
- Specify a return to the 'space for talk' after the action method. If the chairs are arranged in a U shape and the play area has been defined as the extension of the U, then the space for verbal expression is where the participants are seated.
- When the action entails the use of objects or pictures, the creative work space may be represented by a large sheet of paper placed on the floor, ideally in the centre of the semi-circle (or circle) or, alternatively, on a table.

Putting it into words

'Even though we are working in a very small room with tables that are fixed to the floor, we will use as a prop this large sheet of paper that we will place on the table so as to represent the situation with which we are concerned by these symbolic objects'.

Glossary

Cross-references within the glossary are indicated by bold.

Action: Stage 4 of the **ARC** which entails giving oneself over to experiencing a situation, to feeling, seeing, listening and speaking in the **here and now**.

Action facilitator: any person who takes on the role of proposing a specific **action technique** and facilitating it within a **process**. In this book, the process proposed is that of the **ARC**.

Action methods: in this book, we use the term 'action methods' to designate a range of approaches deriving from various practices and theoretical traditions. All these methods draw on movement, experience of the **here and now**, attention to the body and to one's feelings. **Inner attitude** is an important dimension of these methods while, in each case, a specific methodological and theoretical foundation provides the means of accompanying the group process.

Action paths and strategies: Stage 6 of the **ARC** which enables specific actions to be devised and elaborated in pursuit of progress in relation to the **question** under consideration.

Action technique: a specific means of enabling participants, within the **action**, to see a same situation from different angles. In this book, the action techniques presented entail, in relation to an initial **question** or situation, the practice of **role-reversal** and encouragement of physical and spatial movement.

Adoptable: a demeanour and behaviour that enables the other person or the group to feel trust and to take the risk of moving closer.

Analogical Detours: a set of techniques that enable progress to be made through the creation of a symbolic representation. **Metaphors**, **Shapes and Colours**, **Symbolic objects**, and **Similar-sounding Words** are the forms of detour presented in this book.

Analogy: a relationship of resemblance or similarity between objects or experiences possessing some common features. Analogy enables something about the **process** to be read differently, thereby creating links among different levels of analysis.

ARC: acronym signifying the postulate and **process** whereby recourse to *Action methods* opens up the field of *Representations* and thereby enables *Change* to take place.

Brainstorming: a search for original ideas using communication techniques.

'Bring-back' rule: members of the group will ensure that they bring back into the group specific information or exchanges that have taken place outside the official working time and that are worth reporting in the group insofar as they belong to its overall process and dynamic.

Circular question: in the context of a **systemic approach**, modes of questioning that serve to generate change. The **facilitator**, in preparing the circular question, creates **information**. The participants, in their replies, also create information. An example of a circular question would be: 'how would our competitor explain the drop in our turn-over?'

Co-construction: constructing together making use of each participant's **competences** and resources.

Cohesion: the force that brings together and unites the members of a group.

Collective intelligence: a synchronisation, an osmosis, that emerges from a group. Somehow something 'gels'. Synchronisation among persons can give rise to a collective experience and a co-creation that represents something more than the sum of the individuals present.

Competences:capacities, aptitudes, expertise, resources, skills, talents.

Complexity: the nature of what is complex, composed of numerous highly diverse elements.

Connection: anything that, in whatever way, connects or creates links among persons: shared features, similar experiences or expertise, links of whatever kind that testify to the ways in which people are interconnected.

Constructive legitimacy: in the framework of the contextual approach and relational ethics, Ivan Böszörményi-Nagy refers to the notion of constructive legitimacy which represents whatever is experienced as 'fair', in a spirit of 'give and take'.

Context: all the elements surrounding a situation.

Creating information: putting into words aspects of a situation that are present but have not yet been named.

Creative representation: a picture, figure, **symbol**, set of signs that represent a **context**, a phenomenon, an idea or a **question**. Putting together a creative representation is a means of bringing more explicitly into being something that has not yet found expression.

Detour: to make a detour is to travel via a path that is not the most direct route (see **Analogical Detours**).

Discretion: the quality exhibited by a person who understands the distinction between what is *personal* and will remain within the group setting and what is more *general* or *formal* and may be communicated to third parties.

Doubling: a technique developed by J.L. Moreno (1930) in accordance with which one person takes on the role of another, with that person's prior consent, and translates empathetically the experience and feelings of that person. The role-player is careful to check afterwards whether what has been said corresponds to the experience of the person being doubled. The doubling takes place in the first person singular.

Empathy: an inner disposition geared to perceiving what another person might be experiencing, that other person's thoughts, feelings, beliefs, ways of seeing and experiencing what is happening. It is having a 'sense' of the other person, possessing the ability to 'step into his/her shoes'.

Empathy Circle: a technique created by Chantal Nève-Hanquet in the context of which one member of the group plays, with the help of the group as a whole, the role of a person not present in the room.

Empty Chair: a technique used in various traditions of practice to represent a third party not present (person, group, idea, **entity**).

Entity: some form of abstraction. In the **context** of an **action method**, the entity represented may be the company, organisation or other form of system.

Experiment: to agree to live in the experience of the moment by giving oneself over to feeling, listening, speaking and seeing in the here and now.

Explicit: information that may be expressed in verbal or non-verbal form.

Facilitating collective intelligence: creating a **context** within which persons, groups, teams of colleagues and organisations can succeed in finding answers to their own **questions**.

Facilitator: the person whose role is 'to make it easier' to set in motion and direct a process of **co-construction** within the group by paying attention simultaneously to aspects of **inner attitude** and to the questions that are key for stimulating **collective intelligence**.

Fantasy: the faculty of imagination and power of invention that are generated by stepping outside the 'conventional wisdom'.

Field of representations: a dimension opened up to encourage new perceptions of an existing situation, generate the incorporation of new information, and thereby facilitate a broader view of the situation.

Freedom: the rule of freedom states that in a group context, each individual is free to accept or to reject any proposal that is made.

Function: **systemic analysis** uses the notion of function to reach understanding of how what is happening says something relevant about how the system operates.

Genius: the specific form of genius inherent in each person that enables an individual to find unprecedented and original solutions. Talent.

Giving voice to: to take on the role of another person, group, **entity** or concept, either directly or by means of an **empty chair**, an image, or other object, and to speak on behalf of this other person or entity.

Giving voice to the chair: to speak on behalf of whatever or whomever is represented by the chair.

Here and now: all that is ongoing, spontaneous, immediate, of the present moment.

Holding: a concept developed by the psychoanalyst D.W. Winnicott and used here to refer to the way in which a group can gain a sense of its own existence insofar as it feels 'held', 'supported' and 'contained'.

Hypothesis: a provisional explanatory construction based on observation in the **here and now** of some phenomenon or fact. The hypothesis allows direction to be given to an **action** or **(re)search**. It is imbued with observation both external (what is happening in the here and now of the group) and internal (what the **facilitator** is thinking, feeling, experiencing). A facilitator's own theoretical references will influence the hypotheses formed.

Implicit: that which is contained in an expression, a fact, a group or organisational dynamic, and which, without being expressed, influences the **process** underway. This dimension is also sometimes referred to as the **unspoken**. See also **Implicit rule**.

Implicit rule: a term used in the systemic grid to denote a repetitive process that is not given formal expression, that is not mentioned in the **official programme** and yet which is active in the system. Implicit rules say something about the way the system functions.

Inner attitude: a way of being, existential posture, inner availability, and relationship to life.

Interiorisation: the act of establishing contact with an inner dimension, of allowing oneself to feel what is most alive in one's own inner depths. Development of an intimate relationship with oneself. To interiorise something means to assimilate it and 'make it one's own'.

Metaphor: a figure of speech based on **analogy**. The metaphor designates one thing by reference to another, allowing a similarity to be surmised or understood. To achieve its effect as an 'image', the metaphor brings into play **symbols**, colours, pictures, sensations.

Method: a set of interconnected principles and techniques designed to enable a specific goal to be reached.

Mirror neurons: neurons in the brain that become active both when an individual performs an action and when s/he observes another individual perform this action. Discovered in 1996 by the team working with Giacomo Rizzolati, the mirror neurons are linked to the emotional experience of **empathy** and are therefore sometimes referred to as 'empathy neurons'.

Moreno's action methods: the term 'Moreno method' designates a theory and a methodology that is used, on the one hand, for purposes of activating the dynamic of persons, groups, or teams and, on the other hand, for training, academic and social purposes in the corporate sector and a range of organisations and non-profit associations. On the basis of the theoretical and methodological foundation proposed by J.L. Moreno (1930), a wide range of techniques and **methods** have been and continue to be devised. These include **sociometry** and **sociodrama**.

Moreno: in the 1930s the psychiatrist Jacob Levy Moreno created the action method approach now known by his name and based on **role reversal**, **spontaneity** and creativity.

Neurosciences: group of sciences dealing with the study of anatomy and operation of the nervous system. They are frequently presented from the angle of the cognitive neurosciences and research based on brain-imaging.

Official programme: all that is formally announced, clearly and explicitly demonstrated and stated, in a communications system.

One-down position: a stance that the facilitator may choose to adopt in relation to a group or individual group member as a means of seeking to empower the other by expressing a willingness to listen, to admit one's own ignorance in a particular area and to learn from the other who has the requisite knowledge, experience or expertise.

Open Forum/Open Space Technology: a working method devised by Harrison Owen in 1985 in which topics are first decided in plenary session and then working groups are set up to tackle them. Using this technique, it is possible to structure and conduct work on collective intelligence when working with large groups.

Open question: a question that may prompt many different kinds of answer, that acknowledges and welcomes the **complexity** of any and every **context**.

Picture cards: photos, pictures that have been cut out, a set of cards, preferably not containing writing, suitable for prompting a wide range of associations.

Process: deriving from the Latin for 'to move forward', the process within the group represents the evolution of group interactions within a **context**. When speaking of a working method, the 'process' represents the fact that this method is interacting with a context and being conducted in a series of stages.

Prompt: a phrase used by the **facilitator** to encourage a person to play a role. The facilitator begins to say something 'on behalf of . . .' and then the person takes over and continues to play the role in question.

Psychodrama: literally 'psyche in action', the name of the approach created by J.L. Moreno in the 1930s.

Punctuality rule: the requirement to work within the stipulated time frame so as to enable participants to take their bearings in the **context** of the teamwork and to make the requisite organisation in terms of both logistics and psyche.

Question: Stage 3 of the **ARC** during which the facilitator prompts the group to formulate and specify the nature of its **(re)search**.

Reframing: Paul Watzlawick uses the 'reframing principle' to describe the practice of altering one's stance or viewpoint at both a perceptual and conceptual or an emotional level. The same situation will thus be viewed within a different framework which – equally well or even better adapted to the 'concrete facts' of the situation – will change their meaning and significance.

(Re)search: a cyclical action that consists in observing what is happening in the **here and now**, in drawing up one or more **hypotheses**, in selecting a suitable means of intervention, in observing the effects of this intervention, in creating new hypotheses, and so forth. The notion of (re)search is an attempt to render the French '*recherche*' which would usually be translated as either 'search' or 'research', depending on context and meaning. Here, however, both these aspects are relevant. In that consideration of what is being sought is combined with experimentation with ways of achieving it, the French word '*recherche*' is thus able to convey the whole dynamic of the facilitator's work as a constant process of self-questioning in conjunction with ongoing experimentation.

Relational ethic: Ivan Boszormenyi-Nagy defines the relational ethic in the framework of the contextual approach. It is anchored in a principle of fairness and reciprocity among all individuals and in how each person experiences 'give and take'.

Resilience: the ability to 'bounce back' whatever the situation. Facilitation of a group can enable the emergence of new resources and help a group to 'mend itself' after a difficult experience, to give meaning to what is being experienced, and to regain the ability to work and think together.

Resonance: by analogy with the musical term, the way in which members of a group will find themselves touched or affected by other members of the group. It is as if components of individual histories or beliefs are able to be 'brought out' by the encounter with others' histories/beliefs.

Revealing Chairs: a technique deriving from **psychodrama**, thus named by Chantal Nève-Hanquet. A **context** is represented by empty chairs and group members are invited to come to stand behind the chairs for the purpose of roleplaying.

Representational field: the scope and extent of each individual's perceptions, interpretations and feelings about the world. The representational field is imbued with the emotions, beliefs, context and history of each individual. It is enshrined in the dimension of body and senses.

Role Reversal: a technique created by J.L. Moreno (1930) whereby the role of a person, group, concept or entity is first played by another, after which the role-player returns to his/her own role.

Role-taking and de-roling: several action techniques provide for role-playing as a means of seeing and feeling a situation from the standpoint of someone else. A specific procedure is used to facilitate exiting the role and this is sometimes named 'de-roling'.

Safety frame: Stage 1 of the **ARC**. A set of rules designed to foster the creation of trust.

Sense of the other: the capacity to take account of another person and enter a relationship of **empathy**.

Sequential version of a technique: the use of an **action technique** within a defined period of time, as an exercise, with a beginning and an end (cf. **Spontaneous version**).

Similar-sounding Words: this term is used in the technique of that name to refer to words ending in the same sound.

Shapes and Colours: an **action technique** that consists in representing a **question** or a situation by drawing shapes and colours on a support.

Sharing: Stage 5 of the **ARC** during which participants share their experience of the **action** stage.

Sociodrama: an **action method** created by J.L. Moreno that enables people to work on the social aspects of a situation or a **question** with a focus on the social role of each person involved.

Sociometry: created by J.L. Moreno, sociometry is the study of the interpersonal relations of a group, a team, a society, at one precise moment in one precise situation. This technique measures social relations by taking account of attraction and rejection. A procedure known as 'sociometric choice' enables a group to be faced with a choice whereby members are asked to position themselves physically in relation to one another.

Spaces: the space for 'speech' is the place for communication, putting things into words, summing up, devising new paths and action strategies; the space for creative 'play' is where **action methods** are enacted to stimulate the experience of living in the here and now.

Spectrogram: a technique devised by J.L. Moreno that consists in asking participants to position themselves somewhere along a line in accordance with a chosen criterion (seniority, distance travelled to attend the group session, level of expertise in a certain sphere, etc.). In this way, the spectrogram enables members of a group to establish **connections** based on a range of different criteria.

Spontaneity: character of an action that happens 'naturally' or 'on its own'.

Spontaneous version of a technique: the use of an **action technique** whereby small but potentially significant detours may be incorporated into the group work at any point in the **process** (cf. **Sequential version**).

Start-up: Stage 2 of the **ARC**, entailing a warm-up **process** that will encourage **cohesion** within the group for the purpose of achieving **co-construction**.

Surprise: an unexpected event, sensation, thought, or experience that prompts astonishment or wonder.

Symbol/symbolic: any object, image, recognisable shape, word, sound, colour, onomatopoeia, mark, sign, drawing, figure that turns out to be representative of something else.

Symbolic object: a technique that makes use of a wide range of objects of any kind.

Synchronisation: the phenomenon of simultaneous and spontaneous harmonisation of several elements.

Systemic approach: by means of a reading grid that approaches facts about how human beings relate to one another through behaviour and communication in a given situation, this approach focuses on the **context** in which things happen.

Systemic organisation constellations: an approach developed by Bert Hellinger in 1980 and today used in workplace-related settings. By means of different spatial arrangement of objects, this approach enables a **question** to be explored by representing the system within which it arises.

Unspoken: see 'implicit' and 'implicit rules'.

Warming-up: body movements that serve to activate the energy of persons and the group, generally at the beginning of a work session.

World Café: a procedure formalised in 2005 by Juanita Brown and David Isaac whereby participants are asked to move around tables, each of which represents one direction or aspect of the work underway. This method lends itself to work with groups of any size and facilitates the emergence of specific practical and shared proposals.

Resources

Bibliography

Bateson, G. (2002) *Mind and Nature: A Necessary Unity*, New York, Hampton Press.

Blatner, A. (1999) *Acting-In. Practical Application of Psychodramatic Methods*, New York, Springer Publishing Company. (3rd edition).

Blatner, A. (2019) *Action Explorations: Using Psychodramatic Methods in Non-Therapeutic Settings*, Seattle, Parallax Productions.

Boothe Sweeney, L. & Meadows, D. (2010) *The Systems Thinking Playbook: Exercises to Stretch and Build Learning and Systems Thinking Capabilities*, Vermont, Chelsea Green Publishing.

Böszörményi-Nagy, I. & Krasner, B R. (1986) *Between Give and Take*, New York, Brunner Mazel, Routledge Edition.

Böszörményi-Nagy, I. & Spark, G M. (2014) *Invisible Loyalties*, New York, Routledge. (First published in 1984).

Carnabucci, K. (2014) *Show and Tell Psychodrama. Skills for Therapists, Coaches, Teachers, Leaders*, Racine, Wisconsin, Nusanto Publishing.

Carnabucci, K. & Anderson, R. (2011) *Integrating Psychodrama and Systemic Constellation Work. New Directions for Action Methods, Mind-Body Therapies and Energy Healing*, London, Jessica Kingsley Publishers.

Dayton, T. (2004) *The Living Stage: A Step-by-Step Guide to Psychodrama, Sociometry and Group Therapy*, New York, HarperCollins Publishers INC.

Emunah, R. (2019) *Acting for Real. Drama Therapy Process, Technique, and Performance*, New York, Routledge.

Farmer, C. (2018) *Psychodrama and Systemic Therapy. Systemic Thinking and Practice Series*, New York, Routledge.

Hogan, C. (2002) *Understanding Facilitation: Theory and Principles*, London, Kogan Page.

I Ching or Book of Changes (1989) *The Richard Wilhelm Translation Rendered into English* by Baynes C F, Foreword by Jung C G, London, Arkana/Penguin.

Jenkins, J C. & Jenkins M R. (2007) *The 9 Disciplines of a Facilitator: Leading Groups by Transforming Yourself*, San Francisco, Jossey-Bass Publisher.

Jullien, F. (2011) *The Silent Transformations*, translated by Fijalkowski K & Richardson M, Chicago, University of Chicago Press.

Jung, C G. (1995) *Memories, Dreams, Reflections*, London, Fontana Press. (1st edition 1961).

Krall, H., Fürst, J. & Fontaine, P. (Eds) (2012) *Supervision in Psychodrama: Experiential Learning in Psychotherapy and Training*, Wiesbaden, Springer VS- research.

Laloux, F. (2014) *Reinventing Organisations – A Guide to Creating Organisations Inspired by the Next Stage of Human Consciousness*, Millis, MA, Nelson Parke.

Nève-Hanquet, C. (2012) The Use of Psychodrama and Role Playing in the Supervision of Psychodrama Practitioners, in Krall, H., Fürst, J. & Fontaine, P. (Eds), *Supervision in Psychodrama: Experiential Learning in Psychotherapy and Training*, Wiesbaden, Springer VS- research, pp. 165–172.

Nève-Hanquet, C. & Crespel, A. (2019) Using Action Methods to Facilitate Collective Intelligence, in Blatner, A. (Ed), *Action Explorations: Using Psychodramatic Methods in Non-Therapeutic Settings*, Seattle, Parallax Productions, 2019, pp. 51–65.

Nève-Hanquet, C. & Pluymaekers, J. (2008) Psychodrama with Landscape Genogram in the Training of Family Therapists: A Tool for Personal Development and Supervision, in Fontaine, P (Ed), *Psychodrama, Studies & Applications*, Leuven, pp. 133–146.

Nève-Hanquet, C. & Van der Borght, C. (1999) Doubled Chairs in Supervision, in Fontaine, P (Ed), *Psychodrama Training: A European View*, Federation of European Psychodrama, Leuven, Training Organisations FEPTO Publications, pp. 269–273.

Oughourlian, J -M. (2016) *The Mimetic Brain (Studies in Violence, Mimesis & Culture)*, Michigan State University Press.

Pluymaekers, J. & Nève-Hanquet, C. (2008) The Landscape Genogram A tool for Personal Development and Supervision. *Human Systems, The Journal of Therapy, Consultation and Training* 19(1–3) (2008), pp. 212–221.

Rizzato, M. (2014) *I Am Your Mirror: Mirror Neurons and Empathy*, Torino, Blossoming Books.

Rizzolatti, G. & Sinigaglia, C. (2007) *Mirrors in the Brain: How Our Minds Share Actions, Emotions and Experience*, Oxford, Oxford University Press.

Scharmer, O. (2018) *The Essentials of Theory U: Core Principles and Applications*, Oakland, CA, Berrett-Koehler Publishers.

Schein, E H. (2013) *Humble Inquiry: The Gentle Art of Asking Instead of Telling*, San Francisco, CA, Berrett-Koehler Publishers.

Senge, P. (2006) *The Fifth Discipline: The Art & Practice of The Learning Organization*, Doubleday, Deckle Edge, Revised & Updated edition. (1990, rev 2006)

Stephenson, C E. (2014) *Jung and Moreno. Essays on the Theatre of Human Nature*, New York, Routledge. (1st edition).

Watzlawick, P., Helmick Beavin, J. & Jackson, D. (2011) *Pragmatics of Human Communication: A Study of Interactional Patterns, Pathologies and Parad fantasy oxes*, New York & London, W. W. Norton & Company.

Wiener, R. (2009) *Creative Training: Sociodrama and Teambuilding*, London, Jessica Kingsley Publisher.

Webography

American Society of Group Psychotherapy and Psychodrama (ASGPP). Available at www.asgpp.org

Bay Area Moreno Institut (BAMI). Available at www.bayareamorenoinstitute.com

Blatner, A (2019). Action Explorations. Available at http://actionexplorations.com

British Psychodrama Association (BPA). Available at www.psychodrama.org.uk

Federation of European Psychodrama Training Organisations (FEPTO). Available at www.fepto.com

International Association for Analytical Psychology (IAAP). Available at https://iaap.org/

International Association of Facilitators (IAF). Available at iaf-world.org

International Association for Group Psychotherapy and Group Processes (IAGP). Available at www.iagp.com/

Institute of Cultural Affairs (ICA) International. Available at www.ica-international.org/top-facilitation

International Sociometry Training Network (ISTN). Available at www.sociometry.net

Laloux, F (2014). Reinventing Organisations. Available at www.reinventingorganizations.com/

Moreno Museum Association. Available at www.morenomuseum.org/

Presencing Institute. Available at www.presencing.org/

Facilitators possessing a working knowledge of French will also benefit from recourse to the following books and websites.

Ancelin Schützenberger, A. (2008) *Le Psychodrame (nouvelle édition)*, Paris, Petite Bibliothèque Payot.

Ausloos, G. (1995) *La compétence des familles. Temps, chaos, processus*, Toulouse, Eres.

Crespel, A. & Nève-Hanquet C. (2018) *Faciliter l'intelligence collective, 35 fiches pour innover, co-construire, mettre en action et accompagner le changement*, Paris, Eyrolles.

Centre pour la formation et l'intervention psychosociologique (CFIP). Available at www.cfip.be

Ecole Française de Psychodrame. Available at http://ecoledepsychodrame.fr/

Institut Odef. Available at www.odef.ch

Association Belge de psychodrame. Available at www.psychodrame.be

The process does not stop here!
Just visit our website: www.arc-facilitation.com

Index

Note: Page numbers in *italics* indicate figures on the corresponding pages.